Coming Home: Refuge in Pureland Buddhism
by Satya Robyn

Previous books by Satya Robyn

What Helps: Sixty Slogans to Live By

Just As You Are: Buddhism for Foolish Beings
(with Kaspalita Thompson)

Thaw

Small Kindnesses

The Letters

The Most Beautiful Thing

Afterwards

Some Kind of Freak

Coming Home
Refuge in Pureland Buddhism

Satya Robyn

Woodsmoke Press

Coming Home: Refuge in Pureland Buddhism
ISBN: 978-0-9931317-5-2

Published by Woodsmoke Press 2019

Cover photo and design by Kaspalita Thompson

Woodsmoke Press
Amida Mandala Buddhist Temple
Malvern
WR14 4AA

kaspa@woodsmokepress.com
www.woodsmokepress.com

Dedicated to Dharmavidya, my teacher, who showed me the light and who continues to illuminate my life.

Far-reaching is the Light of Compassion;
Wherever the Light reaches,
It gives one joy in the Dharma, so says the Buddha.
Take refuge in the Great Consoler.
~ Shinran Shonin

We have a few hours of precious sunlight. It's cold & fresh &
each bare twig is teaching.
~ Terrance Keenan

Contents

A note on personal pronouns

As foolish beings, it is easier for us to form a relationship with unlimited light when we give this light a form, a story and a gender. Sometimes we connect with this light through an enlightened human being, as was the case with Jesus or with Shakyamuni Buddha. Sometimes we connect with it through a relationship with a more mystical figure, such as Amitabha Buddha or the bodhisattva Quan Shi Yin. A mystical Buddha has the ability to appear in whatever form is most valuable to the seeker.

Behind our human spiritual teachers and our mystical figures is the light, and the light itself is beyond gender. As a way of pointing towards this, and to help us to get out of the bad habit of the generic masculine pronoun, I have made the decision to use 'he' and 'she' interchangeably for Amitabha Buddha throughout this book.

Introduction

Who am I? I am broken. I hurt those I love without meaning to, and sometimes on purpose. I eat too much sugar. I am a teensy bit addicted to Facebook. I tend towards workaholism. I do catch myself more often these days, but I still love juicy gossip. I am sometimes afraid of intimacy and of being in community. I manipulate those around me in order to get my needs met. I make the same mistakes over and over again.

Who am I? I am brimming with wisdom, gratitude and love. I am a successful author and psychotherapist. I am ordained as a Buddhist Priest and I run a thriving temple with my husband. I find my work deeply fulfilling. I have invested in more than two decades of work on myself – therapy, 12 step groups, courses, and thousands of books. I know myself pretty well. I'm not afraid to say 'no' and I'm not afraid to say 'yes'. I am blessed with a very happy marriage, good friends, and a strong community around me. I am full of faith. I have been given a great deal, and I would like to pass it on.

Who am I, and how can I help you? I am an ordinary, foolish being. I am an ever-shifting mixture of the first description of myself and the second; light and dark, deluded and enlightened. And I know that I am acceptable, just as I am. I know it in my bones. This brings me great consolation. I hope this is one of the ways in which I can help you – by reminding you that you are also a mix of awful and wonderful, and that you are also illuminated by the light of love.

As a Pureland Buddhist, the name I use for this light is Amida Buddha, the Buddha of Infinite Light. Being in relationship with Amida has shown me that I am acceptable, just as I am, and that I can relax. Amida knows the very worst of me, and she understands why I am the way I am. Paradoxically, as I feel known, understood, and loved, the sharp edges of my dysfunctions begin to wear away. My defences start getting dismantled, and my fear-driven behaviour becomes less necessary. Being known in this way also keeps me humble, as I come to see the depths of my self-deception and my egoic striving. Finally, it helps me to be more patient and compassionate, as I see these same processes at work in other people.

It doesn't matter to me how you conceptualise your own light or what name you give to it. It would make me happy if this book helped you to discover or remember it, and to experiment with leaning into it. As your faith grows, you will find that you are also more able to be honest about yourself – that you become more courageous and more vulnerable. You will feel more secure, more relaxed, and more content. I'm hoping you'll feel more grateful, more playful, and more joyful. That's how it has been for me.

I would like to offer you the gift of a relationship with the light, through refuge. We will begin with a crash course in Pureland Buddhism, which is the lens I most often look at the world through. Feel free to substitute any of the concepts for those you are already familiar with or feel more comfortable with – 'the spirit of love' for 'Buddha', or 'trust-in-something-that's-not-me' for 'faith'. We'll then look at the five refuges in this school of Buddhism, followed by how to take refuge and what results you might expect when you do. Each section is fleshed out with little stories from my life, which I hope will begin to bring the abstract concepts to life.

Whatever your experience of spirituality, your life history and your world view, I trust that you will find common ground with me. Life is full of twists and turns – and sometimes it knocks us sideways. We all need as much steadying as we can get. I hope that this book will open you up to more of the Buddha's light, whatever you choose to call it, and draw you into a deeper experience of refuge.

What is Pureland Buddhism?

Pureland Buddhism is a form of Buddhism with its roots in the original teachings of Shakyamuni Buddha, the Buddha who was born in India two and a half thousand years ago. It was founded as a separate school in 12th Century Japan, by a Buddhist teacher called **Honen**.

Honen was well known as someone who lived an ethical and highly disciplined spiritual life, but he was repeatedly disappointed by encounters with his own limitations. Honen lived through a time of great turbulence in Japan, with many natural disasters and feudal wars. This chaos was believed to be a result of being in the time of **mappo**. The time of mappo is where the influence of Shakyamuni's teachings had faded to the extent that students could no longer find enlightenment through sustained meditative practices and rigorously following the precepts. This chimed with Honen's own experience of continually failing to meet his expectations of himself. Despite his decades of study and practice, he came to see himself as completely unable to save himself through his own efforts.

It was also true of Honen's time that only a lucky few were able to benefit from Buddhist teachings. You could only seriously practice Buddhism if you were born into the right family, or if you had enough time, money and intellect for extensive study. Honen was determined to find a form of Buddhist practice that was available to and suitable for all, regardless of what class they were in, how academic they were or whether or not they were living a virtuous life. He diligently searched the sutras and commentaries for a solution to his personal spiritual dilemma and to the dilemma of his time.

After reading and re-reading many ancient Buddhist texts, Honen eventually had an epiphany whilst reading a commentary on the Meditation Sutra by Shan Tao. He understood that if we **say the name of Amida Buddha**, we can rely utterly on the power of this Buddha to save us. Amida (in Japanese), or **Amitabha** (in Sanskrit), is the Buddha of Infinite Light. Honen decided to select this practice of saying the Buddha's name as suitable for all foolish beings, and as the only practice necessary to deliver us from the blind passions that drive us. Rather than trying to 'pull ourselves up by our own bootstraps', saying the name opens us up to Amida, who is reaching out towards us from her own side. Amida has the power to lift us up.

The practice of saying the name of Amida Buddha is known as the **nembutsu,** which means remembering (nem) the Buddha (butsu) in Japanese. Pureland Buddhists say or chant the nembutsu in different languages – '**Namu Amida Butsu'** in Japanese, '**Namo Omito Fo'** in Chinese etc. In Amida Shu, my own particular school of Pureland Buddhism, we mostly say '**Namo Amida Bu'**, an anglicised version of the Japanese. 'Namo' can be translated as 'I take refuge in', 'I call out to' or 'I pay homage to'. When we say the nembutsu we take refuge in Amida Buddha - we connect to the spirit of limitless love and lean in.

Some Pureland Buddhists think that we should say the nembutsu as often as we can, and some think that saying it once, with faith, is sufficient. Either way, we can see the nembutsu as the connection between ourselves and the Buddha. We begin like Honen by realising our insufficiency and powerlessness as **bombu** beings - a Japanese word meaning 'foolish beings of wayward passions'. We see that we have no choice but to turn to the Other Power of Amida Buddha.

Amida picks us up, and she puts us down in her Pure Land. This is poetically described in the Larger Pureland Sutra as a beautiful place we go to when we die, with crystal-clear bathing pools, heavenly music and jewelled trees. Some Pureland Buddhists are relieved to be assured of their place of rebirth, and this helps them to feel more settled in their current lives. Others see the descriptions of the Pure Land allegorically, as the perfect field of influence which surrounds a Buddha or any great being full of compassion and wisdom. We are in Pure Lands when we visit a garden planted and tended with love, a bakery owned by a baker who kneads love into their bread, or a home created by a host who is made happy by sharing the best of what they have with their guests.

However we imagine the Pure Land or Amitabha Buddha, we can trust that if we connect with a spirit of limitless love we will be inspired to create our own mini Pure Lands here in this life. Pureland Buddhism tells us that we can lean into this limitless love, and if we do we'll slowly feel the benefits of knowing that everything is going to be alright. We begin to have an experience of knowing that we are loved and accepted by Amida Buddha **just as we are**.

Being in a close relationship with Amida or the spirit of love doesn't solve all our problems, or mean that we don't continue to suffer. It does mean that we find ourselves slowly growing in serenity, equanimity and joy. As we grow in faith, we are given the courage to face our troubles with more dignity. We live more noble lives. Most importantly, more of our energy is released so we can use it to help others – not because we ought to, but because it comes naturally to us. We begin to see others with the eyes of Amida Buddha. We see their suffering, and we reach out.

What is refuge?

Buddhists from all the different schools of Buddhism speak about **taking refuge** in the **three jewels**. These jewels are seen as reliable and trustworthy in contrast to the things we usually take refuge in, such as popularity, money, control, chocolate, possessions etc. The three jewels are:

Buddha – this can be seen as both Shakyamuni Buddha, the great man whose teachings led to the foundation of Buddhism in India two and a half thousand years ago, and the archetype of any enlightened being who has woken up to the truth and has broken free from the fetters of greed, hate and delusion.

Dharma – this refers to the spiritual wisdom of Shakyamuni Buddha and those teachers who came after him. It includes forty years of Shakyamuni's teachings and doctrines, which were initially preserved orally and then later written down and gathered into collections of sutras.

Sangha – this is the community of followers who are inspired by the Buddha's teachings. The Sangha practice together, encourage each other and inspire each other.

As Pureland Buddhists, we add taking refuge in **Amida Buddha** and **the Pure Land** to this list.

Amida Buddha – Amida or Amitabha is the Buddha of Infinite Light and Life. He is also known as the Buddha of All Acceptance. Different Buddhas have different qualities and Amida is like the sun, radiating compassion. He is unimaginably huge and powerful. Amida is often depicted as a red Buddha, and is accompanied by his two attendants Quan Shi Yin and Tai Shi Chih.

The Pure Land – this is the field of merit that surrounds Amida Buddha. It is described in the Larger Pure Land sutra as an exquisitely beautiful and peaceful land where we can easily absorb the teachings of the Buddha. In Mahayana Buddhism, every Buddha generates a Pure Land which is a manifestation of their particular qualities. The Pure Land can also be seen as the field of influence around any great being, or any place that helps to connect us to the sacred.

Just As You Are

We begin here: just as you are.

This is the promise my Buddhist teacher made to me when I first encountered Pureland Buddhism. Amitabha, the Buddha of Infinite Light, loves us like this. Just as we are.

Not when we've self-improved. Not when we finally conquer our out-of-control ice-cream eating. Not in three weeks' time, or even later today. Right here, as exactly this person we are right now.

This doesn't mean that the Buddha doesn't care when we hurt other people, or when we do things that harm ourselves. It makes her sad. She does have a deep understanding why these things happen, however. She sees our history and our particular pattern of wounding, and she gets it. She sees how it is to be human. She sees the love behind the fear.

Are parts of you feeling cynical about what you're reading? Indulge me for a moment. Allow for the possibility that there is *something* out there, wise and compassionate enough to enfold all of our worst dysfunctions in love. Imagine that we don't have to do anything to receive this esteem. Imagine that we are completely seen and utterly accepted.

This is where we begin.

On not murdering anyone

This morning got off to a bad start. Rather than turning on my computer and starting my writing, I turned on my computer and went onto Facebook. My reasons were initially virtuous – it felt important to reply to someone who'd asked for some advice the night before – but before long I was liking posts and getting caught in the infinite scroll.

I was interrupted by Kaspa who popped his head round my door and told me he'd rearranged the chairs in the temple shrine room, two floors up from my office. He said that I might want to look at them later, but I was eager for further distraction, and jumped up. 'I can do my writing later', I thought to myself.

After an hour of fine-tuning where we put the chairs and zafus, we were happy with the new arrangement. I came back down to my office and, after checking for new emails and red notifications, I opened my manuscript. I wrote a sentence. I checked my phone. I deleted a sentence. I wondered if there were any new emails. I went to make a cup of tea. I stared at the screen. I reached for my phone.

As I sat there, I was aware of various voices in the background – "It's my fault for not sticking to my plan and getting side-tracked into furniture arranging." "You don't need to push yourself all the time – you deserve a rest." "It's Kaspa's fault for telling you about the chairs." "You'll never get your book finished at this rate." "You need to give up Facebook." "Facebook is essential for your work as a writer." And so on.

These voices were different parts of me who were trying their best to get my system into a better equilibrium. The striver part was pushing hard against the lazy or avoidant parts. My creative part wanted to write, but other parts of me weren't in the mood or didn't care. The parts of me that use unhealthy coping mechanisms to put out fires noticed that everything was getting a bit heated, and they started to panic. My binge eating part suggested I could eat some biscuits with my tea, and so I fetched three out of the freezer and ate them quickly, crunching through the partly frozen middles.

This is how Kaspa found me when he came downstairs later – sitting miserably in my bucket chair, my kindle on my lap. I didn't even have the concentration to read. He asked me what was wrong. "I'm a terrible person," I told him miserably. "I'm not writing and I ate three biscuits."

"That's okay, you haven't murdered anyone," he said.

It was true that I hadn't murdered anyone. And, in that moment, I really was suffused with the feeling that I was a worthless lump of flesh. I am forty three now. I am no longer a spring chicken. Decades of reading about compulsions, increasing my self-knowledge and practising restraint have left me just where I started – utterly unable to control myself. I find writing just as difficult as I ever did, and maybe even a bit more difficult. I not only ate three frozen biscuits, but I am at this very moment considering eating three more.

I am out of control. And here I am, back at my laptop again, typing away. I think that it was helpful to be reminded that I am not a murderer, even if I felt like one. Kaspa knows me and my various favourite dysfunctions, and he has seen it all before. He knows that sometimes I feel bad about myself, and he also witnesses that I still manage to get up, dress myself and make enough money to feed myself. Sometimes I even do some yoga, and weed the vegetable patch. Once every year or so I start writing a book, complain continually about how difficult it is to write, and eventually finish it.

Kaspa's fond amusement reminds me of what the Buddha sees when I sit there glumly eating biscuits. She doesn't laugh at me, but she certainly has a glint in her eye. "Ah, there she goes again. Turning away from the fear and towards sugar – yes, I can see why that happens, especially with those extra-myelinated pathways in her brain. Oh, and that sad part is in the driving seat again now, the one that feels unworthy. It's a shame she can't feel me shining my love on her, but I'll just keep standing here as I always do. Maybe sooner or later she'll catch a glimpse of me out the corner of her eye."

The Buddha also looks in this way at people who *have* murdered people. The Buddha understands the causes and conditions that led that person to murder or do other terrible things, and it makes her very sad, but she gets it. It is said that there is a Buddha in every hell realm, and that we always have the opportunity to start making better choices, however much of a mess we've made of things. The murderer Angulimala did turn his life around when he met Shakyamuni Buddha in historical India, and it didn't wipe his karma clean but he did go on to live a productive and ethical life. He went on to be happy. The Buddha accepts it all, from minor overindulgence in sugar all the way down the scale to the very worst our race is capable of.

I caught a glimpse of the Buddha reflected in Kaspa, and it was enough to get me out of that chair and back into this one. The worthless part of me is still hanging around, and my stomach is making lots of interesting noises. That's okay – they can sit here with me as I carry on writing. Just as I am.

Purrs and dribbles

When I was a teenager, I worked for a summer at a holiday club for children with learning and physical disabilities. I didn't have any experience of working with children with disabilities, and I felt quite out of my depth. I carefully watched the other young volunteers and the staff in charge for clues about how best to interact with different children.

One morning I was asked to read stories to one of the boys. He was in a wheelchair and couldn't speak. I wasn't sure if this was due to his physical disabilities or because of a learning difficulty. I sat down with him and began to try and work out whether he could understand me and, if so, how much.

I can't remember what my methods were, but I didn't get very far. After a while, the leader of the holiday club walked through the room and I grabbed her. I knew that she'd spent lots of time with this boy and that she knew him well. I asked her about his mental capacity, wanting to choose the right book for his stage of development, and wanting to know whether I was actually communicating with him or just under the illusion of communication.

Her answer was, "It doesn't matter." I can remember being a bit taken aback. She stayed for a while, encouraging me to pick a book I liked the look of, and to read it in an engaging way. I sat next to him and read, and before long his face broke into broad smiles. We chuckled the morning away.

I still don't know how much of the book he understood, and the leader was right – it didn't matter. What mattered was finding a way to just hang out with him, without needing to do a full set of IQ tests first. What mattered was beginning to get to know him, and allowing him to get to know me. What mattered was finding a way of meeting.

By the end of the morning I felt very fond of him. This straightforward appreciation of his essence reminds me of my tabby cat, Tsuki. When Tsuki comes in from her adventures she'll seek me out before she goes to her food bowl and start purring loudly. She usually dribbles. What is it that makes her so happy? What is it that she appreciates about me?

Tsuki doesn't enjoy my presence because I know a lot about the Dharma. She doesn't care whether or not I do any exercise, or if I give money to charity every month. She enjoys it when I talk to her, but not because of anything clever or kind I say. She knows how I look and smell. She knows the sound of my voice. She knows how I stroke her. She takes a simple pleasure in being near me. She purrs because I exist, and because she knows me.

I sometimes forget that this appreciating-what's-there is at the heart of my connections with my friends and loved ones. Maybe I was initially attracted to them because I was impressed by their jobs, or because I found them funny or attractive, but this isn't why I stay in relationship with them. If they stopped being funny or attractive, or got different jobs, I wouldn't sack them. It's not about what they can do for me. It's not about how they make me feel about myself. I hang out with them because I simply appreciate who they are – all the different parts of Caroline, and all the different parts of Alessio.

Amida Buddha sees us as we are, and this is what she loves. She doesn't need us to be a particular way in order to love us. This unconditional prizing is very rare, even in our relationships with our parents or in our partnerships. We are always sizing the other person up – are they cleverer than me or not as clever? Do I find them attractive? What might they be able to offer me? Being the recipient of this means that we also get good at giving other people what they 'want', subtly altering our behaviour in order to go up in their estimation. A woman might learn to flirt with powerful men or to underplay her intellect in order to be accepted. An employee might tell their colleague that they like her necklace because they want her to notice them. We are always adapting our behaviour, noticing how it seems to be going down, and adapting it again.

Coming into relationship with the limitless light cuts through all our attempts at manipulation. We receive our first taste of feeling accepted without needing to pretend or to change ourselves. This includes an acceptance of our continued attempts at manipulation, human as we are. As we feel more settled in knowing that we are accepted by the Buddha, we take our focus away from other people's judgements of us. We come to believe that it is unnecessary to change other people's view of us – as they say in the 12 step programmes, 'what other people think of me is none of my business'.

When we feel accepted, it becomes more possible for us to see our own darkness, and to see what we can do to bring it into the light. If the Buddha sees that we are mean to our little sister, and keeps on loving us, we are more likely to break through our denial and see the truth of this ourselves. We don't change because we think the Buddha will only keep on loving us if we do – there's nothing we can do to stop that love shining at us. We do it because we are in an atmosphere free of blame, and so we can look more calmly and honestly at our choices. The Buddha doesn't need us to become kinder. It makes her happy when we do.

Seeing through Amida's eyes

Earlier, the temple doorbell rang. I have designated today a 'writing retreat day' by creating a rare and precious space in my diary. When the bell disturbed me I had only just got back down to writing after a self-generated distraction, and so the first time I ignored it. When it rang for a second time I hesitated, and on the third ring I reluctantly headed up the two flights of stairs to see who it was. Maybe it was someone delivering the books I'd ordered, needing a signature? Maybe it was a templemate who'd locked themselves out?

Waiting in the porch was a woman with a small dog. As I opened the door she made that swaying movement with her whole body that I've come to recognise. She had decided she was coming inside the temple, and I was in her way. I noticed that she'd already taken her shoes off. I held my ground as I smiled and asked her how I could help her. She explained that she often visits the area, and today she'd decided to pop in and have a look around.

I don't blame people for thinking that we might always be open to visitors. Other Buddhist centres and churches are often open to the public. It so happens that we are a small temple which is also a home to eight people, and my husband and I work from our home offices and are often unavailable. We clearly state our regular opening times on a notice on the front door, encouraging people to return at those times, and we have a second sign on the inside door asking people to ring the bell only if they have an appointment.

Still, a couple of times a week, people do ring the bell. The part of them that is determined to come in decides not to notice the signs. Depending on my mood, this can be a trigger for me. I can't help seeing it as a lack of consideration of our own needs as managers of the temple. Do these people think that we should be continually available at a moment's notice to spend half an hour showing them round? Don't they care about whether we were in the middle of something? These thoughts are swiftly followed by guilt as I reflect on how inflexible and unwelcoming I am. What a terrible priest.

Over time, I have become more skilful at managing these interruptions. Today, I have a brief conversation with the woman at the door, fussing her dog and listening as she talks. She had a troubled look – there was a blankness behind her eyes. I carefully explain when she would be welcome to come back and look round, or to join us for practice, and gave her the leaflet with all our opening times. So far in four years of running the temple these 'drop-ins' have never made it back, but I trust that their intention to engage with the Buddha will continue to urge them forwards at their own pace. Maybe at some point they will return, or go to another place where they might find some of the limitless light. I hope so.

I try to remember to look at these troubling interactions from both sides. On one side was a slightly chaotic person who was too self-centred to notice the signs or reflect on how they might be impacting me. On the other was a slightly uptight person who was too self-centred to adjust her afternoon to make space for a suffering human being. I will continue to work on improving my flexibility, tolerance, and empathy. I will probably also continue to be uptight and protective of my time.

Amida sees both of us, and he smiles warmly at our struggles. He sees the reasons for my uptightness, and he sees the reasons for the person at the door's different struggles. Our behaviour always makes perfect sense when you can look into our personal histories and see the fear behind our carefully constructed defences. It makes Amida sad to see people who are missing opportunities to be compassionate, and to see people who are struggling, but he understands. He doesn't need us to be any different to care about us – he cares about us right now, exactly as we are.

I can't always see people through Amida's eyes. Certain people get under my skin, or frustrate me, or push my buttons like crazy. I know that I have this effect on other people sometimes too. Even if I can't stand these people, I know that Amida cares about them to exactly the same extent that he cares about me. This can be challenging. It boggles my mind that anyone could continue to care for human beings who have chosen to maim or kill others, or even to commit genocide.

Amida can see the suffering behind all these terrible acts. We don't always manage to see rapists and murderers through Amida's eyes, and that's okay – Amida has got it. We don't always feel glad to see others receiving love when we think we deserve it more – Amida continues to love us, resentment and all. When we notice fear or even hate arising, if we can bear to see it just as it is, we can offer it to the Buddha. Something rather remarkable may then happen. Our fear or hate fades and instead we are softened, and warmed. Like a stone soaking up the sun, we can then radiate our heat out to others.

Nembutsu

How can we bring ourselves into relationship with whatever-it-is that accepts us just as we are?

You can see whatever-it-is as the qualities of infinite compassion and wisdom, or as a wholesome energy. You can imagine it as a magical being in a faraway land. You can see it as a benign unfolding process, or the spirit of Gaia. We see it as having the face of a Buddha, and we call it Amitabha.

It doesn't matter how you see Amitabha, or even whether or not you believe it exists. Put your preconceptions to one side for the time being, and act 'as if' something exists that sees you and cares about you. Be curious about what happens next.

Throughout history, people have brought themselves into relationship with this Other in different ways. Some people pray or perform rituals. Some people sit in silent meditation or say the Jesus Prayer. Some people walk in nature or take refuge in groups.

In this school of Buddhism, we use the nembutsu.

The nembutsu is saying the name of Amitabha. Names are powerful. They conjure the energy of the object we are naming. When we say Amitabha, we are connecting to the radiant qualities of the Buddha. We are giving these qualities permission to soak into us.

We usually chant or recite the nembutsu in anglicised Japanese: Namo Amida Bu. Namo means 'I call out to', 'I take refuge in', or 'I am grateful for'. Amida is Amitabha. Bu is a shortened form of Butsu, Buddha in Japanese. Six syllables, a window which light streams through.

The nembutsu is simple, portable, quick, accessible, and powerful.

When we say the nembutsu, whether once or many times, we are opening ourselves up to the power of something bigger than us. We can rely on the power of Amitabha as being infinitely greater than our own. She sees the bigger picture with perfect clarity. She has endless supplies of patience, courage and forgiveness. She never abandons us. We can begin to practice leaning in to her, and trusting her.

The nembutsu is the central practice of Pureland Buddhism: nothing else is required. We say Namo Amida Bu and, in taking refuge, we come to feel that we are accepted just as we are.

Making space for grace

I winced slightly as I set my alarm for 5.45am, so I could join the monks for their morning prayers. I was on a 12 step retreat at Douai Abbey, a Benedictine community in Berkshire in the UK.

After singing praise to God in the peaceful space of the Abbey, the monks slid quietly back to their quarters, and I decided to go on a walk before I went back to my room. It was still early and none of the other retreatants were about. I left the buildings behind me and chose a path around the edges of a meadow. The thick dew gave the grass a ghostly look, and the edges of the landscape were draped in mist. The water seeped in through my unsuitable shoes, soaking my socks.

I followed the path, skirting the field. The grass had been harvested and folded into great rolls which were wrapped in black plastic and dotted across the field. As I walked I sang my own version of praise to God – the nembutsu – chanting 'Namo Amida Bu' over and over. The melody I followed was the one we use when doing prostrations in the shrine room. Whenever I use this tune, the prostrations are with me – my body folding forwards and resting deliciously on the ground to show my respect and gratitude to the Buddha.

I noticed how much clearer my mind was after being on retreat for a couple of days. I hadn't been distracted by emails or the endless list of jobs-to-be-done around the temple. My mind had started to settle, like a cat on a comfy blanket. I stood in the sun and looked out across the open land, lingering before I entered the dark alley of trees that would take me back to where I began. My cheeks soaked up warmth and my whole body soaked in the beauty of this world. How rarely I stop to fully appreciate it. How rarely my mind stays with me, rather than racing off impatiently into the future.

I glanced round to the dark tunnel of trees. Two deer! They were standing in the shadows at the back of the tunnel and watching me very carefully. How long had they been there? They observed me for a few more moments before delicately trotting away, deciding to take a different route to wherever they were going.

The deer were a gift of grace – received only because I paused before I returned to my room, to the mundanities of draping wet socks over the radiator and making my bed. My habit is to rush through the tunnel and get on with my day. My habit is to cram 'doing' into all my spare moments, like pouring fine sand into a jar of pebbles.

We have to make spaces in our lives if we want grace to find an entrance point. We have to set our alarms early and join the monks, chanting in their pure countertenor voices. We have to pause and feel the sun on our cheeks. We have to find a way of opening ourselves up, of making invitations, in whatever ways we can.

These spaces don't have to be a whole fortnight of retreat, or hours of studying sacred texts. We might enjoy doing these things, or feel a benefit, but they are unnecessary. As Pureland Buddhists, all we need to do is say the nembutsu. Every time we say it, we make a space. Namo Amida Bu – here I am, Buddha – little me. Using these tiny invitations, the Buddha stitches his golden thread around us – creating a glittering web that holds us safe. We don't always see it, but as time goes on we trust more and more that it is there.

Different flavours of nembutsu

I try to never miss my breakfast nembutsu. When I open my eyes, the first thing I see is the silhouette of our Buddha statue on our bedroom windowsill. If I remember, this brings the first silent nembutsu: Namo Amida Bu. Next I go to my office, light an incense stick, bow to my golden Buddha and say a short prayer. I then sit in my grey bucket chair with my prayer beads and chant the nembutsu fifty four times.

These five minutes of nembutsu are like a piece of toast and peanut butter for my spiritual self – they set me up for the day. They remind me that I can put the Buddha at the centre of my life, and lean on him regardless of what my day brings. If I skip them, that's okay – the Buddha loves me anyway.

There are many nembutsu snacks sprinkled throughout the day. We usually say grace before we eat, and when we're too impatient for a proper grace, there's always time for a quick Namo Amida Bu to signify our gratitude. I say Namo Amida Bu to greet templemates in the temple hallways, and use it in place of 'see you later' when I leave my husband to go to my office. It often runs through my mind when I catch sight of one of the many Buddhas scattered around the building.

Several times a week we hold formal services at the temple which are open to the public. A service is an hour of different practices – silent sitting, walking nembutsu, prostrations, a Dharma talk, hymns... These services give us a chance to practise the nembutsu more formally, and to practise together. As one of the perks of being resident priest, I either get to run these services myself or to attend those run by my

30

husband or by colleague priests. Some of our congregation attend one or more services a week, some once a month, and if they are further away or if their lives are more complicated, some once a year.

A few times a year we hold longer Buddhist events. We have an immersive nembutsu practice, where we chant continuously for many hours – a banquet of nembutsu. Sometimes people do solitary nembutsu retreats, like going away to an old-fashioned sanatorium and being given a week of bed rest, sea air and good food. Sometimes we have longer retreats which include honest sharing about our lives – a kind of sharing nembutsu – and this strengthens the bonds between members of the congregation. People also have their own private nembutsu practices at home.

The great Pureland teacher Shinran told us that one nembutsu is enough, as long as it is uttered with complete faith. I think that this is true. I also think that, as a foolish and forgetful being, I benefit from frequent reminders of the Buddha. Even though I live in a temple full of Buddha rupas, I continually forget to turn towards the light rather than towards other refuges – too-much-work, too-much-chocolate, too-much-seeking-praise. I aim to find a balance between Shinran's single nembutsu and Honen's advice that we should start with ten thousand nembutsu a day and go up to fifty or even a hundred thousand. Personally, if I set the numbers too high, I rebel and resentment seeps in. On the other hand, if I don't make any efforts to turn towards the Buddha, I get more and more tangled in samsara, this earthly swirl of attachments and karma. I try to encourage myself gently, as you would a child.

Sometimes nembutsu have a very special flavour. The words spontaneously arise when I am knocked sideways by an especially glorious sunrise. I speak in gratitude – Namo Amida Bu. Maybe I utter the nembutsu in desperation as a call for help, Namo Amida Bu, and receive immediate consolation. Once I remember standing in a Cathedral and marvelling at the religious feeling that had inspired such majesty – Namo Amida Bu.

Generally, the nembutsu that move me the most are those that combine with one of the five jewels: Sangha. Five hours into a session of immersive nembutsu, everyone is fading a little when someone I know and love walks in through the door – my eyes well with tears. We ordain a beloved student into the priesthood, and warmth and pride floods through me. I join my voice with Dayamay's for our regular morning meditation session, and imagine the Buddha smiling at us.

So many flavours of nembutsu and, as time goes on, I appreciate them more and more. I pick up new subtleties, and come to appreciate my 'daily bread' nembutsu ever more deeply. I feel that I am saying the nembutsu less out of duty, to be a 'good Buddhist' or a 'good person', and more through gratitude. I see people from different faith traditions performing their own version of nembutsu, and I feel deeply connected to them.

Just three words, and such power. Sometimes these words mean 'please help me', and sometimes 'thank you'. Sometimes they mean 'please remind me that you are there'. More and more often these days, they mean 'I love you'. Amida always says it back.

Small stone nembutsu

Decades ago I invented a form of observational writing called *small stones*. I went on to use *small stones* in the mindful writing company I founded with my husband, Writing Our Way Home, and for many years students wrote *small stones* as a part of our courses.

A *small stone* is a short piece of writing (a few sentences at most) which is the result of paying proper attention to the world. It doesn't matter whether the form is poetry or prose, or what the writing describes. A *small stone* necessitates a slowing down and an opening up of our senses to what is here, followed by a careful recording of whatever is experienced. Here are some examples:

a concentrated drop of light on the Buddha's golden chin

The squirrel draws a delicate wavy line across the lawn with its body and luxurious tail as it heads towards the bird feeder. The rain is soaking everything. Downstairs the hoover screams.

No spaces in the hospital car park: cars circle like vultures.

she tells us again the story of when she met her husband, the story of when the naughty teenagers ran through her garden, the story of the bats, the story of when he was called up during the war. most of the objects in her house are older than me.

last week's baby-pink nerines are half shrivelled, half intact, their narrow petals bending back with extravagance

two
swans
fly
over:
their
long
necks
stretched
straight
out

A couple of years ago, I asked my Buddhist teacher Dharmavidya if *small stones* could be seen as a form of nembutsu. He said yes. This made me happy. I'd had a nembutsu practice for all those years before I became a Buddhist, without even knowing it.

To explore their similarities with nembutsu, I'll look at *small stones* from both sides. The first is from the side of the writer – 'little me'. As a writer of *small stones*, we attempt to see the world as clearly as we can – just-as-it-is, rather than the world we want or don't want. We put aside our preferences and we open ourselves up to an encounter with whatever is here. We trust that something will be there, without us needing to manipulate it. We don't need to work for it, or be 'good'. The world comes forward with abundance, to anyone who asks for it. This is the Pureland Buddhist calling out to Amida without expectation, and with a simple faith.

From the other side, we find that the world calls out to us from its own side. It calls out with beauty – the pop! of that luminous orange nasturtium in late October. It calls out with horror – the rat I thought had been killed and that suddenly wriggled and squirmed, trying to shrug off death, when I moved it from the path. It reveals a multiplicity, a staggering complexity, which should bring us to our knees. It brings us the lessons we need to learn, and it comforts us when we are low on hope.

As we practice writing *small stones*, every day if we can, then we find ourselves snuggling up a little closer to the world. We catch sight of ourselves in its mirrors, and we feel contrition edged with compassion as we see our foolishness. We become less preoccupied with the machinations of our egos, and more able to appreciate the colour of the robin's breast as he pauses in the elder. We begin to imagine that it is possible to lean in to the world, and be held. Try writing *small stone* nembutsu, and see for yourself.

Taking refuge

The beating heart of this book is refuge.

We all take refuge. We take refuge in money, status, chocolate, our homes, our families, people-pleasing, our jobs, alcohol, exercise, controlling people, places and things, our health, our looks, coffee and television.

It would be more accurate to say that we attempt to take refuge in these things, as none of them are reliable or permanent. Some of them are healthier than others, but all of them are ultimately doomed to disappoint us.

As Buddhists we are encouraged to take refuge in the only three things we can ultimately rely on – the Buddha, the Dharma, and the Sangha. As Pureland Buddhists we add two more to the list: Amida Buddha and the Pure Land.

Amida Buddha is a being of infinite light, life and love. We could substitute any source of unlimited compassion and wisdom.

Shakyamuni Buddha is the great teacher who lived in India two and a half thousand years ago. We could take refuge in any accomplished spiritual teacher.

The Dharma is the teachings of the Buddha and all those who followed him. We might also take refuge in any great spiritual teachings.

The Sangha is the community of practitioners who follow the Buddha. It can also be seen as all our companions, from whatever tradition, on the spiritual path.

The Pure Land is the field of merit surrounding Amida Buddha. It is also any place that is made beautiful, peaceful, and supportive of our spiritual wellbeing, through the presence of a great being.

When we begin, we might not know what it means to take refuge in these things, or how we should do it. We give it a try anyway, imagining that we might be able to lean into our new spiritual community, or experimenting with handing over a problem to the Buddha. We take small steps and we see what happens. We feel our way.

We keep on eating too much chocolate, and we keep on messing up.

When we practice taking refuge, sometimes we feel a result, and sometimes we don't. Over time, however, we begin to notice a firmer kind of ground under our feet. We get a glimpse of how it might be to live with the freedom of faith. We begin to find our way home.

Refuge in Amida

Amida, or Amitabha in Sanskrit, is the Buddha of Infinite Light.

Amida is brighter than the sun.

There is a beautiful description of this Buddha in the Larger Pureland Sutra, which lists twelve names as ways of describing the different qualities of this light – The Buddha of Measureless Light, Boundless Light, Unimpeded Light, Incomparable Light, Light of the Monarch of Fires, Pure Light, the Light of Joy, the Light of Wisdom, Continuous Light, Inconceivable Light, Ineffable Light, and The Buddha of the Light Outshining the Sun and the Moon.

This poetry points towards the scope and ferocity of this wholesome energy. How would it be to come into relationship with a power such as this?

Whether or not we are sure that this energy exists, either in the form of Amida Buddha or in a more abstract way, we can experiment with aligning ourselves with it, and allowing ourselves to be influenced by it.

We can know that this energy sees everything, and is stopped by nothing.

We can remember that this light is suffused with joy, which is freely offered to everyone it touches.

We can trust that the light is always there, wherever we go.

We can take refuge in it.

Just like the sun, we can stop this powerful light with something as insubstantial as the thin skin of our eye-lids. If we close our eyes to her, she respects this and does not penetrate. She waits patiently, and is here as soon as we open our eyes.

Amida is here as soon as we open our hearts.

Yowls and deep sea monsters

Yesterday evening I was sitting quietly with my cat Roshi purring on my lap when he suddenly decided that he had things to do. As he leapt off my lap he used his claws for leverage, inserting them into the flesh above my knee. I let out a long cry – yeaaooooowwwwww.

Over the next few seconds I noticed that our other cat, Tsuki, was no longer curled up on the fake fur blanket we leave folded for her next to the radiator. Instead she was skittering around the edges of the living room, her back and tail low, her eyes wide. I realised that she was petrified, and then I realised that her fear had been triggered by the noise I had made.

For half-asleep Tsuki, my yowl had been the cry of a tomcat, itching for a fight. Over the past couple of months our new neighbours' cats had been challenging the safe territory of the temple garden, and there had been some ugly scraps. Tsuki had received a deep wound to her side which hasn't yet healed. No wonder she was terrified. Not only was she woken by a strange cat in her living room, but now she couldn't even see where it was so she could run away from it.

Fear operates on a very primal level in us. My yowl catapulted Tsuki out of her bed, before she even knew what was happening. When an angry elephant starts charging or we see a man with a gun, we don't have time to weigh the options and make an informed decision. Our legs make sure that they get us out of there.

This instinctual reaction reminded me of when I was at the dentist last week. I have a phobia of vomiting (emotophobia), and having dental instruments in the back of my mouth makes my body afraid that I will retch (which has never actually happened). When the dentist asked if it was okay to do an x-ray, which involves biting down on a big piece of plastic which pushes at the back of my mouth, I noticed that my stomach became afraid before I did. The anxiety bloomed and pulsed before I worked out why I was afraid, and it continued after I had reassured my stomach that everything would all be okay.

In my experience, more of our behaviour and our decisions are a result of these primal, instinctual urges than we'd like to admit. We invent stories that make sense of our reactions post-reaction, rather than seeing how little power we have over our minds, our emotions and our bodies. We like the idea of improving ourselves, and we put a great deal of energy into the self-perfection project. We build flimsy structures on the beach and meanwhile great sea monsters roil in the deep, making waves that knock our delicate buildings over in a second.

Refuge affects the very bottom of the sea. By saying the nembutsu we are inviting Amida into relationship with us, and this affects us on a deep level. When we begin we notice some of the more superficial effects of taking refuge, like feeling calmer after we've practiced or finding an answer to a dilemma in a Dharma talk. We can enjoy these effects, and they will encourage us to continue practising, which is a good thing.

These effects can also be seen as the tip of the iceberg. Being immersed in an atmosphere where we feel accepted just as we are, and beginning to trust that we can lean in to something, will cause shifts inside us on a much deeper level. Like shifts in the base of the iceberg, these changes might be slow but they have a disproportionately large effect on what's happening higher up. A centimetre of straightening up or some strengthening deep deep down can result in all sorts of adjustments nearer the top.

We can liken it to the accumulative effects of doing regular yoga. Sometimes I feel a bit calmer or stronger when I've finished my yoga, and sometimes I just feel tired. These are the superficial effects. After a few weeks, however, I notice that I can sit more comfortably in the lotus position, and after a few months I notice that I have got to the top of the steep steps in town without being out of breath. On an even deeper level, the yoga may be massaging my internal organs and improving the functioning of my digestive system. Day by day, I practice yoga because I trust that it is a good thing to do, like brushing my teeth. Taking refuge is the same. We trust that it is having some good effect on us, because someone we trust told us it would, or because we trust our own instincts. We may notice changes in ourselves as a result, but as time goes on we don't get too bogged down in looking for evidence. We trust that the act of taking refuge is enough.

The next time we are dragged out of our sleep by a loud yowl, we find that we don't feel quite so afraid.

What happened to me on retreat

Some years ago I was asked to do a solitary nembutsu retreat as a part of my training to become a Buddhist priest. For three days I would stay in a garden hut at the tiny Amida Shu temple in the centre of London, and spend every second of my waking hours chanting the nembutsu.

Acharya Modgala was running the retreat. It was her job to bring me three meals a day, to make sure I wasn't disturbed, and to check in with me once a day. Apart from that I would see no one, read nothing and do nothing except say or sing Namo Amida Bu.

I can only remember fragments of the days that ensued. I can remember my struggles with the lumpy mattress. I remember my gratitude for how Modgala prepared my meal trays with great tenderness, including treats she thought I might like. I can remember sitting at the bottom of the long, narrow, jungle-like garden and watching the light play with the leaves, making shapes. There were phases of boredom, and flashes of intense claustrophobia at being 'stuck' with myself. I remember the excitement of a visiting neighbourhood cat, and the warmth of the sun on my cheeks.

I am not a person who is used to sitting still. I don't enjoy not-doing for very long, and the absence of distractions was alarming. I took lots of naps as an escape from the intensity of the situation. I wrapped myself in blankets and watched my thoughts come and go. The sound of my voice accompanied me wherever I was, and was a backdrop to whatever was going through my mind. I heard the name of Amitabha Buddha thousands of times.

I spent some of my time wondering about what I was actually doing. To my old atheist self, it seemed ridiculous. I didn't know how much I 'believed' in the Buddha at that point in my life, and I was partly doing the retreat to tick it off the list. At least some of my reasons for wanting to be a priest were of the propping-up-my-ego variety. I wanted to be the sort of person who went on retreats. I had more wholesome reasons for wanting to do it too; a trust in my teachers, and a genuine curiosity. A few colleagues had told me stories about their own nembutsu retreats, and I had to admit to being intrigued by the fragments they shared. As they talked, their eyes shone. I wanted to know why.

This mix of boredom, napping and sun on my face wasn't quite what I was expecting. It all seemed very ordinary. On the third day, I finally settled down into not needing anything to happen. Shortly afterwards, I was lying on my back on the lumpy bed. My body went tingly, and I was flooded with energy. I went slightly outside of my body as something came down and peeled layers off my heart. It happened three or four times – zhooom, zhooom, zhooom.

The intensity soon faded, and I was left feeling mildly surprised, intrigued, and pleased. I felt a little raw and vulnerable, but not too much – it was as if the layers were a scab that was ready to be discarded, or winter clothing shed in a warm room. When the retreat came to an end, I knew that something within me had changed forever. It wasn't the sort of shift that leads to revolutionary changes in one's life. I wasn't

44

suddenly planning to leave my job, or go on pilgrimage to Japan. It wasn't like the miracle of a caterpillar changing into a butterfly.

It was more like falling in love. There was less between me and everything-else, and so I felt everything a little more intensely. The greens of the garden were greener, and the scent of the roses was extra-delicious. I wanted to smile more. I was more tender, and the world hurt me a little more. Over the following weeks and months these effects mostly wore off, but the layers had been peeled off, and there was no way of sticking them back on. My heart had been opened.

Was it Amitabha who peeled the layers from my heart? Was she responding to the many hours I had spent calling her name?

Who knows. When we are in the realm of spiritual experiences, there are no guarantees. I'm sure my experience could easily be explained away at a physiological or psychological level, rather than a spiritual one. If that's the explanation that others would favour, that's okay with me.

What I do know is that this experience, wherever it came from and however I make sense of it, helped bring me closer to the Buddha and closer to the world. It offered me a deeper refuge. Nothing has been the same since.

A Ready Brek glow

In the UK we have a breakfast cereal called Ready Brek, which is made of finely ground oats with added flavouring and vitamins. The idea is that you serve it hot, so your child can go out into their day warm and charged up with energy. It became popular in the 1980s because of a now iconic advert. In it a cool young boy (the sort of boy we all wanted to be) sits at his breakfast table and, as he spoons the Ready Brek in, a warm orange fuzz develops all around his body. He jumps up, full of energy, and as he skips his way to school a postman is so shocked by his radioactive glow that he almost falls off his bicycle.

A few years ago, I became aware of my own Ready Brek glow. We were holding a Buddhist service in our old house, in our small living room. As preparation for moving into the temple, we spent a few weeks offering the same schedule we planned to offer when we moved, seeing if it felt doable. I think there were just three of us there that morning – Kaspa, Wendy and myself. We approached the silent meditation section of the service and sat quietly, my back to the glass doors which opened out onto our long garden.

I was drifting between thoughts when I was gifted the vision of a warm, holding force-field all around me, following the contours of my body perfectly and moving when I moved as if it were a wetsuit. The difference between my glow and the Ready Brek glow was that between me and this warmth there was a millimetre or less of space.

This space was the respect that the Buddha paid me. He didn't want to force himself on me, but instead was always

46

there, hovering just a little distance from my skin, inviting me to lean in. With this image came the knowledge that, if ever I wanted to, I only had to move a millimetre in any direction to feel held by the power of the Buddha.

Do we need to eat Ready Brek or do any special spiritual practices to develop this spiritual glow? I don't think so. I see the infinite light as surrounding everyone, regardless of what kind of person they are or whether they are aware of it. I see it reaching into the darkest prisons and into places of war and famine. I see it accompanying a person from their first few cells (maybe before?) to the very end (maybe after?). I see it staying close, regardless of how furious we are at the world or how many heinous acts we commit. I see this light as truly unconditional.

There are conditions to our making contact with this light. We need to take refuge. We need to relax to the extent that we are no longer clenching our muscles so tightly, holding ourselves up or together. We need to lean back into the water and know that we won't sink. We need to trust that if we step off the top of the hundred foot pole into mid-air, the Buddha will catch us.

The Buddha can't force us to do this, just as we can lead a horse to water but then have to step back and let the horse's thirst do the rest. Even if the Buddha could, he wouldn't want to. He wants us to choose refuge. He wants us to put the cereal into our own mouths, and taste it for ourselves.

Of course, it is scary to step from the top of a hundred foot pole. We find that people often first visit the temple when they have run out of other options, when they are feeling desperate enough to try something that might make them vulnerable. It is the same with clients coming for psychotherapy – it is never at the top of anyone's list of possible solutions. We often have our first encounter with our Ready Brek glow when we are at the end of our tether, when everything else is falling apart.

Sometimes we are lucky enough to choose to lean in before we reach the very limits of our self-power. Either way, after that first taste, it is necessary to practise leaning in over and over again. Before long we will realise that we have gone back to grabbing at other refuges instead – status, money, alcohol, being in control and all the rest. When this happens we can attempt to loosen our grip and find our way back to trust. Sometimes we will manage this and sometimes we won't.

Whether or not I am able to choose to relax, it comforts me to remember the image I was given. It's better than a Ready Brek glow. The light of the Buddha is closer to me than I can imagine, and it will never leave me.

Refuge in the Buddha

Amida Buddha can sometimes feel too huge for us to take refuge in. We imagine ourselves as a speck of black on his coat-sleeve, and we disappear.

Siddhartha Gautama was a prince who was born around two and a half thousand years ago in Kapilavastu in India. His mother died as she gave birth to him, and his father was overprotective and spoilt him. His existential questioning led him to leave the safety of the palace and he became one of the greatest spiritual teachers of all time – Shakyamuni Buddha, the enlightened one.

We can put ourselves in relationship with this historical figure, who passed on his wisdom with great generosity for forty five years. His teachings fill many fat books. We can also access his spirit which has been passed down from teacher to disciple throughout the centuries, tended carefully like a flame. His spirit is alive.

Shakyamuni Buddha is also a window through which we can form a relationship with any of the many Buddhas. Each Buddha or Bodhisattva (beings who delay their own enlightenment so they can help others first) has its own particular qualities – the courage and creativity of Tai Shi Chih, or the great understanding of Manjushri. If we are in need of gentleness, we can go to the great mother, Quan Shi Yin. If we are sick we can call on Bhaisajyaguru, the Medicine Buddha.

Whether we are taking refuge in a Buddha or in an avatar from another great tradition, we put our small selves aside for a moment as we open ourselves to a bigger wisdom.

49

We imagine what the Buddha might have said, or we dwell for a while in the force-field of the Buddha's great kindness. We put our burdens down, and we lay our heads on his golden lap.

We take refuge in the Buddha, who is always there.

A Buddha in every hell realm

Sometimes life feels hopeless. Maybe we are struggling with an addiction, or our hearts are breaking. We might feel trapped in a stressful job, squashed by the pressures of supporting our family, or we might have retreated into a prison of depression or bitterness. Maybe someone did terrible things to us and we can't find a way out of their shadow. Maybe we have done terrible things and we can't find a way of forgiving ourselves. Maybe there hasn't been any light for a long time.

Inhabiting these spaces can feel like being in hell. The descriptions of the hell realms or Narakas in Buddhism are enough to make your hair stand on end. In the Devaduta Sutta we hear:

"Then the hell-wardens lay him down and slice him with axes. Then they hold him feet up and head down and slice him with adzes. Then they harness him to a chariot and drive him back and forth over ground that is burning, blazing, & glowing. Then they make him climb up and down a vast mountain of embers that is burning, blazing, & glowing. Then they hold him feet up and head down and plunge him into a red-hot copper cauldron that is burning, blazing, and glowing. There he boils with bubbles foaming..."

The graphic horror of these descriptions can be seen as the Buddha using skillful means to dissuade people from making bad choices - a warning that if they do, they will end up somewhere terrible after death. I also see them as a way of describing the bad spaces we can inhabit in our present-day lives. How else could we describe the pain of a father who has sexually abused his daughter, or a child in a time of war who has lost her whole family?

When we have a run of bad luck or when we make a series of bad choices, especially when we are already burdened with heavy karma, we will end up in a hell realm. We are in a hell realm when we spend our days straitjacketed by anxiety, or when we isolate ourselves and float aimlessly without connecting to others. We all pass through hell realms and we may stay in them only briefly or be stuck there for a very long time. Bad luck or unskillful choices lead to worse conditions, which often result in more bad choices – the circle circles ever more viciously.

The good news is that there is a Buddha in every hell realm. Buddhas such as Ksitigarbha travel between the hell realms, acting as a guardian and a guide for the inhabitants of these terrible places. I like to imagine him sitting calmly in the corner of the cavern full of tortured souls, shining golden, waiting patiently for anyone to come up to him and ask him for help. Maybe he's even offering to help but the beings in hell realms have their fingers in their ears...

Sometimes it is hard for us to leave our own versions of hell, despite how little sense that seems to make to us or to those around us. We can see this illustrated in small ways – we persist in overeating regardless of how ill it makes us feel afterwards, or we continue to be mean to our brother-in-law even though it makes us miserable. We would somehow prefer to feel the familiar pain than to encounter the alternative, which might mean becoming vulnerable or overwhelmed, losing our security or comforts, facing up to the terrible things we've done, losing someone or simply stepping into the unknown.

I have seen people emerge from the most terrible of circumstances and radically change their lives. These changes often begin when they finally realise that they cannot do it on their own. They turn to a Buddha – a therapist, a 12 step programme, a meditation practice – and they allow themselves to be helped. They lose faith in their self-will and instead become open to grace.

Sometimes we need to suffer a great deal before we are ready to break open. There is no way of knowing how long we will stay in our hell realms. We can see others dwelling in hell realms too – our loved ones, our enemies, whole countries. It may seem that we will be there forever, but we should never write anyone off, including ourselves, however much pain they/we are in and however much pain they/we have caused others. Change is always possible. If we have experienced this salvation ourselves, we should remember to tell others, so that they will also have hope. There is a Buddha in every hell realm. The Buddha forgives us, and he is patiently waiting for us to come back to him.

Looking away from the screen

My stomach was fizzing with anxiety. It was Thursday evening and I was preparing to do my first live broadcast of a Buddhist service on Facebook. I run several services a week at the temple without any nerves, but this was the first time I'd led a practice session online, and it felt different.

Partly I was nervous because lots of contacts had expressed interest in attending – students from other schools of Pureland, an admired colleague, friends who didn't know anything about my work as a priest. What would they think? Partly it was because I wouldn't be sat in our shrine room looking at the whites of my congregation's eyes, but broadcasting out to the world, without knowing who was watching or how they were reacting. I was worried that I might get the liturgy wrong or dry up during my Dharma talk. I felt vulnerable.

I was cross-legged on the small patch of carpet behind my desk, my computer balanced on my office chair in front of me, and my bookcase shrine behind me. There were ten more minutes before I went live. As the nerves continued to multiply, I realised that I was looking straight at my own face, 'reflected' in the preview of the live video. I had been fiddling with my scruffy hair, noticing the fear in my eyes, and generally feeling preoccupied with myself.

I made an effort to look instead into the eye of the camera at the top of my laptop screen. As I gazed at the black computer pupil, I imagined that I was looking into the eyes of the people who'd be watching and practising with me. This helped my nerves immediately. I started to think about what they might need – who would they be? How could I explain the nembutsu to beginners in a way that made sense? What could I share about my own experience that they might identify with?

Then I noticed my golden Buddha. He was just behind me and so also on the screen, floating above my left shoulder. He sat calmly and peacefully, perfectly grounded. Here was an even better place to rest my eyes. I began to absorb his calm, and to see myself as a tiny part of a much bigger picture. I remembered that when I did my Dharma talk I could step out of the way and let the Buddha speak through me. He knew better than I did what was needed.

When I went live a few minutes later, several friendly names appeared in the comments screen before I began. For my Dharma talk, I shared the story I've just shared with you. Afterwards we all chanted together – I couldn't hear them, but they could all hear me, and we knew that we were chanting the nembutsu in Brighton, in a small village in Essex, in Baltimore, in Croatia. Our voices joined together in the sacred space we were creating.

Amida Buddha's light is powerful. Once I'd stepped out of the way, with my understandable fears of being rejected or looking stupid, the light reached through Facebook and into the houses of my online congregation. I took refuge in the Buddha on my bookshelf, and he filled me up with a grace that overflowed.

A human Buddha

When Shakyamuni Buddha was newly enlightened, he realised that because the people of his time delighted in attachment, were excited by attachment, and enjoyed attachment, it would not be an easy task to convince them of the benefits of relinquishment. He came to the conclusion that they simply wouldn't understand, and that it would be tiresome for him to waste his energy attempting something impossible. He decided to settle into 'dwelling at ease' rather than teaching the Dharma.

Brahma Sahampati, the king of the heavenly realms, saw the Buddha's thoughts and became alarmed. He knew how much the world needed the Buddha's wisdom, and he couldn't allow the calamity of him giving up before he even started. He manifested in front of the Buddha and kneeled before him, exhorting him to change his mind. He said, using that beautiful phrase, that there are a few people who have 'little dust in their eyes', and that these are the ones who will understand. The Buddha was brought up short by Brahma's speech. He looked around with compassion for all beings, seeing that there were those who would benefit from the Dharma, and he resolved to do all he could to pass on what he'd received (SN 6:1).

I love this part of the story of the Buddha's enlightenment as it shows him at the very beginning of his awakened state, at the peak of his powers, and yet he still needs encouragement from Brahma to do something that feels impossible. It points towards the Buddha's vulnerability. It reminds me of the stories of Jesus when he left the queues of people wanting his help to go and spend time meditating alone in the mountains, or the time when the Buddha's assistant Ananda managed to change the Buddha's mind about the merit of including women in the Sangha. It shows us our great spiritual teachers as fallible human beings.

Dharmavidya presents Shakyamuni Buddha in this way in his wonderful book, 'The Feeling Buddha'. We read of a man who isn't perfect. "He did not put himself above us. He was a man who never claimed divinity." Instead he showed us what to do with our suffering. "The Buddha taught enlightenment. He did not teach us that we will never be depressed. He taught us not to be defeated by it. He did not teach us how to avoid suffering. He taught us to meet affliction and live nobly, so that suffering was not unnecessarily multiplied." He took the path of the noble ones, and he continues to inspire us to do the same.

Why am I so reassured to hear about the flaws in my teachers? It's not because it props my own ego up when they get things wrong (okay, maybe just a bit). It's because it allows me to connect with them as incarnate beings, as made of flesh and blood just as I am. If the Buddha sometimes refuses visitors when he needs to rest, then maybe it's okay for me to do that too. If Jesus learnt to read and write in the way we all do, by making mistakes and learning to correct them, then it is okay for me to make mistakes.

When I think of Amida, I find it difficult to imagine any character defects within all that infinite light. I can be inspired and humbled by her vastness, and rest with all my foolish nature in her golden lap. When I come into relationship with Shakyamuni Buddha, however, I can see both the man and the light beyond the man. Shakyamuni knew how it was to live in a world of suffering. If he was able to take the noble path, then maybe I can follow in his footsteps.

Seeing our great teachers as human can also help us to form healthy and realistic relationships with the teachers who guide us in person or through their writings. I have recently discovered the theologian and psychiatrist Gerald May, and am in the process of absorbing his wonderful spirit and wisdom. In his book 'Addiction and Grace', he begins by admitting that he is 'riddled with addictions', some of which he enjoys very much. I laughed at this, recognising the truth of it, and rather than discouraging me from reading the rest of the book (why bother if he couldn't 'solve' the problem of addictions in his own life?) I listened even more carefully to what he had to say.

We must always find this balance of trusting our teachers to take us further than we are able to go by ourselves, and trusting our discernment when we feel uncomfortable about the teaching we are receiving. All human teachers are channelling the infinite light, and as human vessels they are all a little cracked. They all have blind spots. When my teachers are able to recognise and laugh at their own fallibilities, I am reassured. If the Buddha made an occasional mistake, then who are we to think ourselves better than him? We can relax into making mistakes, being human, and knowing ourselves to be accepted as we are.

Refuge in the Dharma

The Sanskrit root of the word dharma is "dhri" which means to support, hold, bear, maintain or sustain.

We can lean into the Dharma, and it will hold us.

What is it? Dharma is a word with a rich history, and it plays a central role in Hinduism, Sikhism and Jainism as well as Buddhism. Amongst other things it describes a universal law or order, ethical behaviour in line with this law, and the path of righteousness.

In Buddhism the word is most commonly used to refer to the teachings of the Buddha. We can immerse ourselves in this wisdom by reading the sutras. These are the words that came from the Buddha's mouth, memorised by his followers, passed down, and recorded as soon as writing was invented.

We can also soak ourselves in teachings given by scores of disciples-turned-teachers since the Buddha's lifetime, including those who are alive today. The Buddhist canon is an open canon, and Shakyamuni's inspiration continues to bring life to new Dharma.

Which teachings do we follow? We can test these teachings out in our own lives and see which are helpful. Do they make sense? Do they give us courage? Most importantly, do they help us to be kinder?

We can allow the Dharma to take us a little bit further than we would venture alone, and then a little bit further again.

We can lean into the Dharma, and it will sustain us.

A rucksack full of greed

Yesterday I arrived at my week's writing retreat at The Clockhouse in the Shropshire hills. I had been anticipating it all month, wondering what my fellow writers would be like, and whether I would manage to finish my novel as I hoped.

I brought with me a heavy black rucksack full of greed. I had chocolate biscuits, posh crisps, marzipan, treacle biscuits, nuts, fruit bars, lemon and cardamom chocolate...

After unpacking I met my fellow writers who were both lovely, and both very successful in their fields. I came upstairs to my room and the questions started. How successful am I in my field? Should I have been successful in their fields instead? As a Buddhist, should I be worrying about how successful I am at all? Is my writing as good as their writing? Am I as good as them? Am I?

I turned to my rucksack and cracked open the chocolate biscuits. I went online and got lost. By the end of the evening I was miserable. I couldn't imagine ever letting go of any of my favourite compulsions – I just seemed to get one under control and another one popped up. I was so disappointed at the gap between the way I want to behave and the way I actually do. I was so tired of carrying the great weight of my metaphorical rucksack of greed, hate and delusion, which comes with me everywhere.

I sent a few messages to friends asking for support, and before I went to sleep I asked the Buddhas for help. What was the answer? How can I be a better person? How can I solve this once and for all?

In the morning, an answer came to me when I was practising nembutsu. The answer seemed to come from outside of me, from a bigger wisdom that has more of the pieces of the puzzle than I do. It felt like Dharma.

The answer: You have your black rucksack with you because at the moment you need it. You feel too vulnerable without it. Maybe in the future you will be ready to leave it at home – but don't worry too much about that now. What really messes with the quality of your days is the compulsive internet checking and browsing. Let me help you with that for now, and don't beat yourself up when you eat too many chocolate biscuits.

And so this morning I have recommitted to checking my email and Facebook just once a day, which has worked so well for me in the past. When I manage to do this, my days open up like the sweeping fields I can see from my desk here. I am no longer tugged around by an insistent need to receive affirmation, or distracted by red notifications. I am free.

This morning I've done some yoga and written some of my novel and it's still early. I need to be careful when things go well like this. I start feeling smug, and the hope springs in me that I could be like this all the time, if only I tried hard enough.

The Buddha smiles at me indulgently when I have these thoughts. I know from previous experience that I will continue to be bombu, a foolish being. I will have good days and bad days. I will feel centred and calm and full of faith, and then I will get jealous again, or lie to look good, or eat too many chocolate biscuits.

A blue tit just swooped down and perched on the outside of my window frame. His feet scrabbled on the glass, and he looked inside the room with his beautiful shining eye. 'Come back into the present!' He said. 'Look! Look at all this!'

I will continue to make mistakes and to fail myself and others. Life will be shot through with suffering. Right now, I am happy.

The teacher appears

In this modern age we are very lucky to have access to so much Dharma. If I click away from my manuscript right now, all I have to do is open a new tab and type in the name of anyone I want to learn from. I can find PDFs, podcasts of Dharma talks, translations of sutras and online communities who are discussing the Dharma.

Sometimes this abundance of Dharma is a blessing, and sometimes it is a curse. As I glance to my left, I can see a towering pile of books next to my bookshelf – the majority from my most recent book-buying frenzy. I realise that I can use Dharma as I would any other drug, by getting my fix, and hoping that this book will be the one that gives me all the answers.

Recently I have been reading Gerald May. Like all the best finds, I came across him by following an unlikely trail of breadcrumbs. He was a psychiatrist and the half-brother of Rollo May, and in his writing he combines his psychotherapeutic wisdom with a deep grounding in his Christian faith. I love his encouragement to release ourselves from the tyranny (and false comforts) of self-will and relax into something bigger. I am also heartened by the soft and forgiving attitude he takes towards the worst of himself. He is speaking to exactly the place that I am in right now, and saying just what I most need to hear.

They say that when the student is ready, the teacher appears. The Dharma works like this. If I'd picked up his books a decade ago, their religiosity would have left me cold. A couple of years ago, and the control freak in me would have baulked. Right now, I'm ripe for his message. I find that the Dharma shows itself to me in a myriad of ways. It may be that I find a new author like May, or meet a new wise colleague in my work life. I may hear a book recommended by three different people in a week, or watch a nature documentary and find it shedding unexpected light on a dilemma. Sometimes the weather is the Dharma, as I see the clouds rolling across the sky and remember that my bad mood will pass.

I tend to find that, when I become more open, more of the world becomes Dharma. If I see someone as stupid, I'm unlikely to hear anything useful from them. If instead I see them as a fellow human being with pockets of dysfunction and pockets of wisdom (sometimes in the same pocket) I find myself feeling consoled or inspired when they talk about their own life. If I carry a question around with me and stay open, I find Dharma in dreams, through watching my bunnies interact, on the radio and in the cobwebs on my ceiling.

I don't always hear the answers when I want to hear them, and they aren't always the answers I want to hear. Dharma isn't a quick-fix solution to all our problems. Sometimes it takes a long time for us to be ready to hear a particular answer, and sometimes the answer can feel more painful than the question. When we 'live our questions' as Rilke suggested, it is helpful for us to go gently. We trust that it doesn't work to force things, and we trust that the answers will reveal themselves as we become ready to see them. We remember Teilhard de Chardin's beautiful prayer and 'Above all trust in the slow work of God'.

In our spiritual lives there is a delicate balance to be had between self-discipline and surrender. I use several structures as ways of inserting Dharma into my days. I do nembutsu practice every morning, and I do a daily reading from the sutras. This gives me a nudge towards the things that are healthy for me, like brushing my teeth and going on a daily walk. I also sometimes catch myself ploughing through a 'worthy' book on my afternoon off, as if I'm taking medicine. I don't think Dharma can flourish in us when we take it as medicine. There are no straightforward rules here – some people will benefit from adding more discipline to their lives, and some will benefit from loosening up. We can ask ourselves, is this taking me towards or further away from the Buddha? Is it taking me towards intimacy with myself, others and the world, or away? Also, what is realistic today – what are my limits?

Engaging with the Dharma is more like painting a picture on a huge canvas than putting together a piece of flat pack furniture. A picture emerges over time and we will change our brushes and colours depending on what is needed. There is no 'right' or 'wrong'. If we can, we watch out for the picture the Buddha has in mind, but she also has a broad taste in art. She wants us to paint the most beautiful picture we can paint, and that will be different for every person. She appreciates all our efforts as if we were her children, bringing home a splodgy mess from school. She wants us to find our own way, using the guidance of her Dharma. Most of all, when we enjoy our painting, it makes her happy.

Eavesdropping on the Buddha

This morning after letting the bunnies out of their hutch I settled into my grey chair for ten minutes of hanging out with the Buddha. I pulled my thick brown Anguttara Nikaya from the bookshelf and opened it to my bookmark on page seven hundred and eighty.

Shakyamuni Buddha taught in India for around forty five years – from when he became enlightened underneath the Bodhi tree at the age of thirty five, to his death at eighty. We have no written records from the Buddha's lifetime, but stories from his day were transmitted orally from monk to monk. We don't really know when they were first written down. Most of the older writings we have are from the Therevada tradition and are called the Pali Canon.

The Pali canon consists of forty volumes, and has been roughly estimated to be eleven to thirteen times as long as the Bible. The Buddha did a lot of teaching in his lifetime. His stories form a rich tapestry, before we even consider the many commentaries from wise teachers throughout the ages. These forty volumes are divided into three sections or 'baskets'. The first is the Vinaya, consisting of stories of how the rules for the Buddha's monks and nuns came to be the way they are. The second and largest section is the Sutras, a collection of discourses by the Buddha and his disciples, and it is subdivided into five nikayas or collections. The third is the Abhidharma, a collection focussing on Buddhist philosophy and psychology.

My first experience of the Pali cannon was during my time training to be a psychotherapist at The Buddhist House,

66

the old home of my Buddhist teacher Dharmavidya. We stayed in the house for the duration of the course blocks, and Monday nights were sutra study for the resident Buddhist community. I sat in the comfy living room and watched as Dharmavidya read from a huge volume. The language was unfamiliar, a little like listening to Shakespeare. He would pause every so often to chuckle generously.

Some people find reading the Nikaya Sutras a dry experience. I feel lucky that my introduction to them was through a man who took obvious relish in their content. Dharmavidya presented these ancient writings as relevant, interesting and often amusing, and I sometimes still hear Dharmavidya's voice in my head as I read.

The Sutras include a lot of repeated passages, and a lot of standard opening paragraphs or sequences, partly to make memorisation easier and partly to really ram certain messages home. If you can accept this, and maybe even learn to enjoy the comfort of the repetition, then you will find all sorts of wisdom in the Sutras that applies to your life today.

A couple of weeks ago I read a couple of teachings (AN 5:161 and 5:162) on how to deal with resentment. One gave several excellent suggestions on what attitude to take towards those you feel resentful towards (including having compassion towards them, paying no attention to them, and remembering that they have acted as a result of their karma and will generate further karma as a result). The other advised relating to the 'good' parts of people we feel resentful towards, paying attention to their good qualities and paying no mind to their unskilful behaviour. We should do this even if we can only find a

67

small amount of the 'good' parts of people, like 'a little water in a puddle'. When dealing with people like this, the Sutra tells us to kneel and put our mouths to the pure water, 'suck[ing] it up like a cow', so as not to stir up the mud around it. Cows often need to drink from muddy puddles, and so have to develop some skill if they don't want mouthfuls of earth. We too need to develop skill in finding the good in people and relating to this.

Some sutras have stayed with me as they remind me of something I often need reminding of. One of these is the Sedaka Sutta from the Samyutta Nikaya, which stars the bamboo acrobat's assistant. The bamboo acrobat erected a bamboo pole and asked his assistant to climb up the pole after him and then onto his shoulders, which she did. He then said that he would watch out for her, and told her she should watch out for him, and that way they would both complete their act and come to no harm. She disagreed with him vigorously, saying that instead he should watch out for himself, taking care with his own footing, and she would take care of her own balance, and that this would be safer for both of them. The Buddha agreed with the assistant in this case, and this story reminds me that sometimes we need to pay attention to our own 'balance' rather than focussing on or interfering with someone else's.

The Pali cannon is full of delightful quirky details that bring the Buddha's stories to life. After reading the sutras for a while, I do feel like I've been hanging out with the Buddha. I can't help but see him as wearing a wry smile sometimes, as he deals patiently with the endless variety of people who come before him. We can't be sure that these conversations between the Buddha and his students were recorded with complete accuracy, and that's okay. Some of the norms in the society of the Buddha's time don't chime with my own values – for example, the attitudes towards women. That's okay. I take what I like and leave the rest, whilst staying open to sometimes changing my opinion. Even when what I'm reading doesn't seem to relate to anything in my own life, I imagine that I'm sitting in the presence of the Buddha, absorbing his wisdom and his great love. Maybe one day I'll finish the Nikayas, which means I can start reading them all over again.

Refuge in the Sangha

The Sangha is the community of spiritual students who follow the Buddha's teachings.

We can find refuge in any group of people who follow principles that help them to live good lives. I take refuge in my 12 step Sangha and my 'friend' Sangha (including those of different religions) as well as my Buddhist Sangha.

The Sangha can be a motley bunch. All human beings have pockets of dysfunction, some broad and shallow, some deep. Sometimes we know about our dysfunction and own it, and sometimes it is completely in our shadow.

It can be dangerous to lean into someone's shadow. This person may tell us that they are doing what they're doing to help us, and completely believe this to be true, whilst unconsciously being driven by self-preservation and potentially causing us harm.

This is why we take refuge in the Sangha as a whole, and not in any one person.

When relationships get complicated, and we wonder whether it is healthy for us to be in them or not, we ask the Buddha, and we ask trusted friends for their advice, and we slowly feel into our own intuition. We try to work out what parts of the difficulty are under our control, and what bits aren't. We learn to say no when we need to, and we wait to see what happens. It can get complicated as we are complicated beings, and we can get thoroughly tangled with each other at a deep level.

Despite this, learning how to be in relationship is a great foundation for living a spiritual life. We learn how to ask for help and how to be honest about our struggles. We learn from watching others. We learn how to reflect on and take responsibility for our own part in tangles. We learn how to be vulnerable.

Refuge in the Sangha can be an advanced practice. When it gets too hard, we can retreat for a while and recoup by leaning into the other four refuges.

Over time, it gets easier. We feel safer, and the tangles happen less often or are less complicated. We learn to trust the people who are capable of (mostly) being trustworthy. We also see our own foolishness more clearly, and learn to be kind to it, and so learn to be kind to the foolish parts of others too.

We lean into Sangha, and a hundred hands come out to catch us.

On being silly at the dinner table

Every Friday evening, the temple residents eat together. The people who live here are more or less involved with the Buddhist activities here, and so this meal gives us an opportunity to meet with each other at least once a week, in this big building where we might go for days without bumping into each other. People take turns to cook a vegan meal, and I usually fail to refuse a second portion.

The conversation tends to be light. We tell each other bad jokes and we make up puns. We tease each other with fondness. It has somehow become a tradition that we play a game where we all guess the answer to a random question – how long does it take frogspawn to turn into frogs? How many billionaires are there in the world? How many flavours of crisps are there? – before asking Google for the answer. This can lead to intense competition...

I sometimes experience moments of self-consciousness when guests from outside of the temple join us for these meals. What will they think of us? Should we be discussing the Dharma, checking our behaviour against the precepts, or eating in contemplative silence? Should we be a bit more Buddhist-ish and a bit less, well, silly?

It was a relief to read Jean Vanier's 'Community and Growth', which describes life in his L'Arche communities for people with developmental difficulties and those who support them. He says that where he lives, when they have oranges with their communal meal, it has become a custom to throw the peel at each other afterwards. He speaks of the delight of suddenly finding a curl of orange peel on one's nose. This once even happened when a Bishop was present. He says:

"True belly laughs are important in community life. When a group laughs in this way, many pains are swept away. Laughter is something very human. I am not sure if angels laugh! They adore. When human beings are too serious they become tense. Laughter is the greatest of relaxations. And there is something funny about humanity. Little as we are, poor as we are, with all our 'animal' needs, we are called to become more than angels; brothers and sisters of God, the Word made flesh. It seems so ludicrous and wonderful, so crazy and yet so ecstatic. And the most rejected are called to be at the heart of the Kingdom. Everything is upside down. No wonder some people at sacred moments have the giggles."

There is plenty of seriousness here in our community. The Dharma is at the heart of everything we do. We bow to each other in the shrine room, and we greet each other warmly with 'Namo Amida Bu' in the hallway. The shrine room flowers are arranged with care, and the same care is taken when we water the plants, clean the guest toilet and hoover the carpets. We touch into these sacred moments when we eat too – when we say grace at the beginning of the meal, when we ask each other how we are doing, and when we help each other to clear away the dirty dishes.

But if they throw orange peel at each other in Jean Vanier's inspiring communities, then I shall continue telling bad jokes without compunction. I will fondly remember the time in service when the celebrant got something wrong and we all broke into giggles and couldn't stop. I shall trust that there is a time for lightness, and that belly laughs leaven our community here. One of the things that most attracted me to my teacher, Dharmavidya, was the frequency of his hearty chuckle. Maybe others will be drawn to the Dharma by our silliness. Have you heard the one about the Buddhist hot dog seller?

Finding shelter in a sometimes-scary world

Next week I will be travelling to Sheffield for a five day training course in a form of psychotherapy called Internal Family Systems. I imagine myself in the group of thirty participants, all experienced therapists, led by a trainer I haven't yet met. As part of the course we'll all be working with our own material in small and larger groups, exposing the vulnerable parts of our psyches to almost-strangers.

I think back to the other groups I've been a member of. My original therapy training, twenty years ago. The first 12 step group I attended. My Buddhist psychotherapy training. The community of Amida Shu Buddhists I met in Narborough nine years ago and who I now see as my second family. My training group to become a supervisor. Arriving into all of these groups was scary but, after time, I began to trust that the other members did care about me and want me to grow. These groups became, within the usual human limits, safe spaces.

In a letter to her mentor Thomas Wentworth Higginson, the poet Emily Dickinson wrote, "Dear friend, I felt it shelter to speak to you." What a beautiful phrase. How do we find the shelter that Dickinson is speaking of in our everyday lives? How can we find the people, groups and places that become our havens?

When we are in an unusual situation or a new group of people, our usual instinct is to hoist up our defences. We are very careful about what we share, how we share it and who we share it with. We have good reasons for this. All of us have been hurt by others in the past. In his book 'Love and its

Disappointments', Dharmavidya suggests that human love is impossible without a measure of disappointment. We are rejected, misunderstood, ridiculed, ignored, manipulated or judged. Our challenge is to find a way of handling this without protecting ourselves from possible future pain by shutting others out.

We might shut down by holding back from saying we felt upset with our friend for being so late, because we're afraid they might get annoyed and reject us. Maybe we never admit to being jealous or vulnerable, as when we were growing up we were ridiculed or shamed when we admitted to these ordinary feelings.

One way of finding shelter is to notice these instincts to protect ourselves when they arise, and experiment with taking a little risk instead. When we keep our defences up, it is more difficult for people to see us and come to care about us. It is also difficult for us to feel truly safe, because we haven't tested what happens when we reveal ourselves. The way to find shelter is to tentatively speak our truth.

I remember doing this with my supervisor training group. Everyone else in the group apart from me had completed their therapy training with the same organisation. I spent the first day feeling like an outsider, and also with the conviction that my training had been far superior to theirs. I decided to take a risk and share my feelings of separateness and superiority with the group, even though it felt shameful to admit. I blushed as I said it. After I spoke, other group members shared their own truth by admitting to a fear of being judged, or by revealing their impatience with others in the group.

As we listened to each other, nobody tutted or asked anyone to leave. As people felt heard and accepted, the group began to feel like a safer place. We created shelter for each other and as we continued to be honest the shelter got cosier and cosier.

On the way to finding shelter, we sometimes get bruised. We might share something and feel judged by the other person. Someone might misunderstand us or talk over us. It might feel like the group is ganging up against us. These dynamics are likely to be a mixture of our 'stuff' and other people's 'stuff'. Our 'stuff' consists of our historical triggers, for example being particularly sensitive to being judged for the way we look or feeling criticised around male authority figures. It also includes the roles we set up for ourselves in groups, usually mostly unconsciously – we might always find ourselves the target of the group's anger or pity, or being the one who isn't taken seriously. Other people will also have their own 'stuff' and might be triggered by people who act like their mother, by conflict or by power imbalances. We are all human beings and we all have our strengths and our shadows. It is inevitable that we will meet difficulty in relationships, especially when those relationships become deeper or more intimate.

It helps to remember our own flaws when we encounter them in other people. It also helps if we acknowledge when we've been bruised and wonder about what we need. This might mean we speak about our experience in the group, or that we reflect on what happened with someone we trust. It might simply mean retreating and licking our wounds for a little while.

More than anything, it helps to remember that there is a bigger container than this particular group. This bigger container holds us safe. The container is the Sangha as a whole, and it is also the Buddhas, the Dharma and the Pure Land. When individual people let us down, we can continue to take refuge in the other four jewels. We can remember that we are supported in numerous ways, even when it doesn't feel like it. The sun is still shining, even if the clouds are heavy and grey.

The shelter is all around us, really.

Why joining communities is so hard

I am a member of several different communities, and I'm sure you are too. Some of these groups are tighter, like my small group of close friends, and some are looser, like my 12 step community, or the members of our Sangha who rarely visit but remain connected. I see creating community as one of my biggest responsibilities in my role as a priest – secondary only to introducing people to the Buddha and Dharma. Sangha is one of the jewels of Buddhism because it is difficult for us to continue on a spiritual path without colleagues and supporters around us.

Over the years I have witnessed many people visiting our temple community for the first time. We watch them as they meet more established members of the Sangha, try out the Buddhist practice we offer here, and begin to orient themselves in a completely new environment. Getting through the door to attend a first Buddhist service is a big deal for most people, but I've come to see that returning for a second time is an even bigger deal. First visits don't involve any commitment – they are a dipping of a toe into water. A second visit is where people begin to play with the idea of joining our community.

When we connect with existing communities, issues inevitably arise. Once we've found the time, energy and motivation to fit something new into our lives, and once we've decided that we can accept the broad philosophies or aims of the group, then the difficulties get more complicated. We can see finding a new group as being like dating, and committing to a group as being like moving in together or getting married.

After the honeymoon is over and once we start really getting to know each other, there are all sorts of disappointments to come to terms with, needs to negotiate, and tangles that need untangling.

Jean Vanier talks about the difficulties in joining communities as fitting into four categories. He is speaking here about joining a tight, intense community like his L'Arche houses or a monastery, but I think these descriptions can also help us to understand our difficulties in committing to the looser communities we all belong to.

"These are the four great crises of community life. The first – which is certainly the least hard – comes when we arrive. There are always parts of us which cling to the values we have left behind. The second is the discovery that the community is not as perfect as we had thought, that it has its weaknesses and flaws. The ideal and our illusions crumble; we are faced with reality. The third is when we feel misunderstood and even rejected by the community, when, for example, we are not elected to a position of responsibility, or do not get a job we had hoped for. And the fourth is the hardest: our disappointment with ourselves because of all the anger, jealousies, and frustrations that boil up in us."

We don't want to let go of who or where we were before we joined, or relinquish the coping strategies we've always used to deal with life. We discover the failings of the community. We feel rejected or feel like the community doesn't understand us. We have an intense encounter with our own failings. When I first read this list, I felt the relief of not being alone. I can identify with all these different crises, both as a new group member myself, and in what I see when others encounter our Buddhist community.

How can we work through these crises when they arise for us, and help others to negotiate them? The most important point is to recognise them as a natural and appropriate consequence of our moving towards intimacy with a new group. We might not encounter all four difficulties, or in the order that Vanier lists them, but there is an inevitability in their arising. It doesn't mean that we are failing when we or others meet these obstacles, but rather that we are on the path of deepening commitment. Remembering this can be helpful both to group leaders and to new group members.

It can help us and others to have a space where we can talk our feelings through without having to worry about being judged or persuaded into seeing things in a particular way – sometimes the group leader can manage this, and sometimes they can't and someone else is more appropriate. I have found that patience is important – here in our Buddhist community we have often had group members who disappeared for a year or more before coming back to continue with their journey. We also need to remember discernment when investigating our difficulties. Sometimes they are showing us that we'd be better off elsewhere. Sometimes we're called to stay where we are, even if that is very painful, so we can learn what we need to learn.

It isn't helpful for group leaders to jump to the conclusion that a group member's dissatisfaction is all their fault. As group leaders it's always important to prioritise the wellbeing of our group members, and to examine what we're doing and make changes when appropriate. It's also helpful to remember that when a new member has complaints about our group it can be more about them and their safety than about our community. This is also true when we are the person complaining. We don't have to control everything or 'make everything okay' for group members. We can have faith that everyone is on their own path. If we leave a community because we are avoiding an aspect of ourselves, this will happen again when we next join a group (and again and again, until we see what we need to see in ourselves). This is true for others too.

Communities are precious places. They help us learn how to love one another and to receive love. They can also be intense and potentially dangerous to the parts of us which are too fragile to protect themselves, or too brittle and defended to learn the necessary lessons. We should always be gentle with those who encounter issues in community, and take the long term view. Keep welcoming group members, encourage honest dialogue, and hand the rest over to the Buddha. We can do the same for ourselves. Living in community can work miracles on us, and we never know when the fruits of this work will appear.

Refuge in the Pure Land

Good people radiate goodness.

They are naturally kind to the people around them, who are kind to others in turn. They take care of their physical space, planting flowers and arranging simple objects artfully, and this inspires others to do the same. They radiate joy, patience, and a sense of being relaxed, and if we spend time in their presence we come away feeling more joyful and relaxed ourselves. Their goodness is infectious.

The field of influence around a Buddha is supercharged, and it is known in Buddhism as a Pure Land. Amida's Pure Land is described extravagantly in the Larger Pureland Sutra as being studded with sparkling jewelled trees and luxurious bathing pools. Exquisite music floats through the air and refreshing breezes scatter petals that fall into beautiful patterns and designs. Everyone who goes there is soaked in peace and bliss. "Delight is everywhere."

When we take refuge in the Pure Land, we are assured that after our death we will go to a good place such as Amida's Pure Land. Even if we can't be completely sure of what this means or whether we can believe it, we trust that our teachers have faith in the Pure Land, and we begin to notice that we feel calmer about our death.

We can also take refuge in Pure Lands in this life, by going to places that have a special spiritual significance to us, or where we feel more connected to the Buddha. This might be the ocean, a garden, a Cathedral, or our local Buddhist group that meets in a shabby room on a busy city street.

We can create mini Pure Lands too, by planting a herb garden, helping to redecorate our village hall, or simply picking up rubbish when we come across it.

We take refuge in the Pure Land, whether it actually exists in the far-away West as it says in the sutra, or if we find a mythical Pure Land in our hearts. In the Pure Land we can relax into knowing that we are washed in the love of the Buddha.

On preparing for death

At the end of my last therapy session, during which I had spoken about how busy I had been and how full I felt, my therapist surprised me (and herself) by saying I shouldn't forget to 'prepare for death'. These three words cut through my worry and flurry and left an empty space. I'm still holding them in mind, wondering at their effect on me and about what they have to teach me.

As a writer I love the musicality of language, and I became curious about the sound of the phrase. Death. It's an abrupt, cutting word – it doesn't have the softness of the longer 'errr' in birth or the spaciousness of breath. Or maybe these are just the associations I'm bringing with me. How would it be to learn to love the sound of the word 'death'? To see the 'e' sound as clean, cleansing, and to hear the final 'th' as a gentle fading away into silence?

As Pureland Buddhists we are told that, if we say the name of Amitabha Buddha, we will go to the Pure Land when we die. The Pure Land, where leaves are made of gold, silver, lapis lazuli... It all sounds very pleasant in the sutra, but there are three problems. The first is that I don't want to leave this life I have now. The second is that I'm afraid of the process of dying. The third, difficult to admit to as a Buddhist priest, is that I'm not always sure I believe in the Pure Land.

I don't want to leave my life as Satya for lots of reasons, and if I investigate them I see that they are all because of clinging. I don't want to leave my loved ones – my husband, family, Sangha, friends and beloved pets. I don't want to leave work unfinished – this book, for example, and the vegetable patch project, and the temple. I don't want to stop enjoying the things I enjoy – expensive chocolate caramels, and the view from the top of the hill, and music, and Bonfire Night, and peonies and redbush earl grey tea and watching long-tailed tits on the bird feeder. And here's the biggie – I really like being Satya. Being Satya is great – most of the time – it's the ultimate balm to my ego. What would be the point of being if I wasn't being Satya? I don't want to be anyone else.

All this clinging would be eased if I had more faith. Faith is the opposite of fear – it allows us to receive whatever is present without grabbing at it, or pushing it away. I am attached to chocolate because I am afraid of being stripped of this easy access to comfort, which helps me to avoid uncomfortable feelings. I am attached to my loved ones because I am afraid of my grief, and of revealing my dependency on them. I am attached to being Satya because I am afraid of letting go into emptiness. The Buddha reminds me that this emptiness is absolutely full of love.

My second two issues, being afraid of the process of dying and of not believing I'm going to a good place when I die, would also be solved by an increase in faith, as would any other problem you can think of.

I am afraid of the process of dying – of feeling ill, of vomiting (this is my biggest phobia), of being in pain, of being completely powerless and dependent and feeling trapped and not being able to escape. What do these fears consist of, if I break them down? When we are ill it is certainly unpleasant – not being able to breathe through a snotty nose, or feeling pain whenever we swallow or move. But experiencing unpleasantness doesn't scare me. What scares me the most is being out of control, being vulnerable, and trusting others.

Augusten Burroughs wrote a comforting book called 'This is How: Surviving What you Think you Can't', and in it there's a chapter about the death of his partner from AIDS. The thing he feared the most was the progression of the illness beyond certain crucial points. How would they cope when there was a loss of bodily functions? A reliance on oxygen? Feeding tubes? He said that what happened in practice was that the new 'awful stage' simply became normal before very long. You imagine that you won't be able to bear it when some new deterioration happens, and then you do. Of course the process of serious illness or dying is accompanied by feelings of distress, pain, depression, rage etc. There are times when these feelings are overwhelming. These times pass, too, and new ways are found of coping with the new reality.

So what about not knowing if the Pure Land really exists as it is described in the Larger Pureland sutra? In one of our core texts, the Summary of Faith and Practice, Dharmavidya writes: "The primary practice requires only one essential: realise that you are a totally foolish being who understands nothing, but who can with complete trust recite "Namo Amida Bu"; know that this will generate rebirth in the Pure Land, without even knowing what rebirth in the Pure Land truly is." The phrase 'without even knowing what rebirth in the Pure Land truly is' helps me to relax, because it gives me permission to keep an open mind about the Pure Land.

I can grow in faith by simply saying 'Namo Amida Bu' and allowing something mysterious to happen. I can listen to and trust my teachers – Dharmavidya and those who came before him, and spiritual teachers from other schools or traditions. I can also pay attention to my own experience. As time has gone on, I have felt a growing sense of okayness about what happens after death. Maybe the Buddha was wrong and when I die I'll disappear completely – fade away into nothingness. In that case, whether I've let go of being Satya or not, then there's nothing to worry about. Otherwise I can trust that I'm going to a good place – who knows what kind of good place, but somewhere where I will be safe and at peace.

I am very much at the beginning of my encounter with the spiritual instruction my therapist gave me. Preparing for death encourages us to wonder at where we're going, and more than anything it brings our attention to how we are living our lives. One of the verses from our Nien Fo book reads:

"While still young and strong, let us each hear the Dharma. Let us strive and diligently seek the path to eternity."

There are many Buddhist texts like this, reminding us that our time is limited, and that while we are here we should make efforts to cut through to what is important. It's easier to be courageous when we are not afraid. Taking refuge in the Pure Land will help us to live more vibrant and joyful lives.

My blue bench

From where I sit, here at my desk, I can see out of my office window to a blue bench. It sits in front of a wall of elderflower and hazel threaded with ivy, a rambling rose and the occasional bramble. Alongside it are the anemones that flower extravagantly in late summer, and the raspberry canes I allow in small numbers so I can strip them of their curling leaves and feed them to the temple bunnies.

In front of the bench is our vegetable patch, which is currently mostly full of squash – butternut, and a round speckled variety I can't remember the name of. As you sit on the bench the temple is on the right, and so over to the left is The View. You can see for miles across the sweeping Severn Valley. It's currently layered in skeins of mist, and it changes every day – clear and sunlit, or decorated with clouds, or fading to dark evening purples as the yellow lights start glowing one by one.

I call it my blue bench, but I must confess that it is actually a pale sage. When we went to buy the paint last year there was no cornflower blue left, and so I chose this colour which turned out to be insipid and uninspiring. I painted it lovingly, just as I had twice before in its proper colour. All those slats, like rib bones – the front, the back, the sides... turned upside down, turned back the right way... two coats. I painted it because if I didn't it would rot, and also because I was grateful to it.

This bench is my portal to a little Pure Land. It has kept me comfortable on baking hot days when I have to take off my cardigan, and on freezing days when I drink tea with my gloves on. It has reconnected me to something bigger when I have got tangled up in my little hurts. It is where I meet great teachers through books, and have conversations with myself though my journal.

We can find or make little Pure Lands like this wherever we go. Here in my office I have set up a shrine on the bookshelf just to my right, and in the living room next door we have fairy lights in our fireplace which I have watched twinkle for hours. There are two pots of bright red cyclamen just outside our back door, and blue lobelia flowing from the urn in the gravel garden – this is enough for a Pure Land. We don't need lots of time or money, or great artistic flair. We just look around us with love and see what needs cleaning or tidying.

We can visit Pure Lands that others have made too. Our friend's jumble of clashing colours and unusual objects might not give us pleasure if we lived in it all the time, but we can appreciate its energy as we sit with a cup of tea. We can appreciate the care and attention that the Japanese gardeners have paid to each tree, each shrub, each fallen leaf – even if we prefer things to look a little more unruly in our own garden. Each Buddha creates their own unique Pure Land dependent on their own qualities and inclinations, and we can see the people around us as doing the same, even if the only evidence we can find of their loving attention is their careful choice of a new hat, or the effort they put into their hobby.

Creating Pure Lands can bring us joy, even if the way is not always smooth – the bedroom paint that turned out to be a shade too luminous and needs to be painted over, or the drought which shrivels two of our favourite acers. They can be seen as natural extensions of ourselves, and there are no rules. One of the greatest pleasures in creating Pure Lands is seeing others enjoy them, as when I invite my gardener friend round to see progress in the garden here, or cook a lavish Sunday lunch for the templemates. We don't need to worry about how 'well' we're doing (although of course we sometimes will).

When we are looking with the right eyes, we begin to see Pure Lands everywhere. This inspires us to create beauty of our own, and the virtuous circle continues. Now, it's time for a break – I think I'll carry my cup of chicory out to the blue bench...

The most exquisite music

Last night something happened that wrenched tears from me. They drew lines down my cheeks.

This something was the sound that came from Awantika. Her voice was the crystal-clear water of rockpools, and a swallow doing precise aerial acrobatics. She was singing love songs to the divine. She *was* the divine.

In the Larger Pureland Sutra there is a description of the beauty of the Pure Land, and this includes the music floating through the air. In Dharmavidya's translation of the text it says:

"An earthly monarch enjoys one hundred thousand kinds of music. From the realm of a wheel turning king up through each succeeding heaven the music of each higher realm is a hundred million times superior to that of the realm below. However the music of the highest heaven improved a hundred million times would not compare with a single sound produced by one of the jewel trees of Amitayus' realm. Moreover, in that land, there are thousands of varieties of spontaneous music and every one is the sound of the Dharma: clear and soft or deep and resonant, they form the most exquisite music, foremost of all the sounds of the ten regions of the universe." (From 'Amida's Land is a Realm of Utmost Joy', 59.)

Awantika, singing in our shrine room, produced these sounds. Alongside her were musicians who have spent decades immersed in the language of this traditional Indian music. It has soaked into every cell of their bodies. They watched each other carefully as they played. They were having a conversation about the meaning of the universe. They were making love.

By the end of the evening I was full of inspiration. Being in the presence of these craftspeople inspired me to take my craft as a writer more seriously. I hadn't been writing *small stones*, a daily practice of writing short observational pieces. This is my version of doing scales, and I began again the morning after the music.

Awantika and her voice also reminded me of qualities I admire and don't embody often enough – humility, unselfconsciousness, decisiveness and grace. She also modelled a completely unapologetic approach to devotion. I have been inspired afresh to move towards these qualities, by following Awantika's example.

Awantika's music touched me at the base of my soul. It reminded me of what is at the centre of everything. I came away fed.

How do we take refuge?

If it is a good thing to take refuge, then how do we actually go about it?

Like arriving at a clearing in a forest, there are many ways to reach refuge. We might walk to the clearing every day by following a path along a river, as a daily spiritual practice. Maybe a spiritual teacher acts as a guide – someone who is familiar with the terrain and who has travelled further than we have. Sometimes we have to take many, many wrong paths and exhaust them all before the clearing appears, through a true encounter with our limitations. Maybe we put on a new pair of glasses and see to our surprise that we are already there. Or we may step into the helicopter of an Other Power, acknowledging that we can't find it ourselves, and trusting it to carry us directly there.

Even one visit to this magical place – one experience of deep refuge – will be enough to sustain us. Once we've seen the truth, we can't un-see it. Having said that, as foolish beings we are easily persuaded to forget what we've seen. The worldly world calls to us like a gaggle of sirens, offering alternative refuges – money, sugar, compulsive sex, success, fame. It takes courage to resist the temptation to take the 'easy' road, which is, of course, never easier in the long run.

Taking refuge is a practice rather than a final destination. Every time we visit the clearing, we get to know it a little better. We receive a little wisdom, comfort or courage to help us on our way. We get lost when we look for it again, but maybe not for as long. We begin to notice what activities bring us closer, and which take us further away. We find companions on the path. We notice how much more quickly we find refuge when we stop seeing the whole business as under our control.

In this section we'll look at some of the ways we can take refuge. Hopefully they will help you on your own journey to the clearing. It's so beautiful there.

Taking refuge through practice

When we practice, we are putting some time aside to hang out with the Buddha.

Different Buddhists do this in different ways – by meditating, by reading sacred texts, or by making offerings. In our school of Buddhism, the primary practice is the nembutsu. As we've seen, Dharmavidya told us in the 'Summary of Faith and Practice' that:

"The primary practice requires only one essential: realise that you are a totally foolish being who understands nothing, but who can with complete trust recite 'Namo Amida Bu'; know that this will generate rebirth in the Pure Land, without even knowing what rebirth in the Pure Land truly is."

Practice begins as an act of faith. We have no hard evidence that it will make any difference to our lives. Sometimes it continues in this way for some time. We carry on brushing our teeth, trusting our parents and our dentists who tell us it will prevent cavities. We carrying on practicing, trusting the Buddha and our spiritual teachers.

As time goes on, we do begin to notice changes. When we start our morning with five minutes of nembutsu, our days do feel a little more spacious. When we miss our weekly hour of practice, we notice ourselves becoming grumpy or out of touch with ourselves. Maybe we start noticing that we are being more patient with our children, or we begin to feel feelings that we'd been burying for decades.

We all need to find our own way with practice. We can practice informally, when we catch sight of the Buddha in our kitchen and give him a bow, or say 'Namo Amida Bu' when we see a dead bird on the road. We can practice more formally, when we gather with the Sangha for immersive nembutsu practice, or when we offer our bedroom Buddha a stick of incense every evening.

Practice is anything that brings us closer to the Buddha. We know when we're closer because we feel less scattered, less alone, and less self-protective. We know we're further away when we feel controlling, important, worthless, tight or dissociated. It's not always so easy to tell. Sometimes, when we move closer, we experience great rivers of sadness welling up. Sometimes, when we move away, we feel alive with buzzy compulsivity. It might help you to discern the difference if you ask yourself, do I feel more or less able to love others? Do I feel more or less able to relax? Do I have more or less faith?

Practice shouldn't become another stick you use to beat yourself with. Give yourself permission to find your own way towards a sustainable practice, or let the Buddha lead you there. Experiment. See what feels wholesome, and what feels like too much of a push. Change your routine when it needs to change, and remain responsive. Notice when you get into comparing or oughting. Encourage yourself, and find spiritual friends who can travel the path with you.

Relax, and enjoy hanging out with the Buddha.

The power of words

One simple way of taking refuge is to say that we are taking refuge. In my tradition, we recite the five refuges during our services using these words:

I take refuge in Amitabha, the Buddha of Infinite Light – Namo Amitabhaya
I take refuge in the Buddha, the one who shows me the way in this life – Namo Buddhaya
I take refuge in the Dharma, the way of understanding and love – Namo Dharmaya
I take refuge in the Sangha, the community that lives in harmony and awareness – Namo Sanghaya
I take refuge in the Pure Land, the perfect field of merit – Namo Buddhakshetraya

I have repeated these words many times, and each time I do, I feel that they have an effect on me. They are a reminder that I have already taken refuge. They also state my intention going forwards, that I will continue to be led by the five jewels, and know them as a place where I can rest.

Saying things out loud is different to saying them in our head. In Alcoholics Anonymous, there is a huge leap between admitting to ourselves that we might have a problem and saying 'My name is Jane and I am an alcoholic' to a room full of people. There is something about hearing ourselves speak and being heard by others that makes our words more real. It's more difficult for us to hide from the truth.

As a part of our Buddhist marriage ceremony, Kaspa and I were surprised when Dharmavidya included a section we'd taken out, where we were meant to read out our personal vows to each other. We hadn't written any, and here we were, standing in front of a hall full of waiting family and friends. I opened my mouth and started crying. I was so grateful to be marrying this man.

There was something about this invitation that was hugely powerful. I was being asked to put my intention to marry Kaspa into my own words, and then to say them out loud in front of the people we loved. I stuttered some words out through my tears, and heard the ones he said in return, and we both felt like the heart of the ceremony had been completed.

We can see reciting the refuges as a mini-marriage ceremony. We are making a private or public vow to rely on the Buddha, Dharma and Sangha, and to prioritise these refuges above all other. By taking refuge in these immutable objects, we are loosening our refuge in what is impermanent – having a successful career, people-pleasing, cigarettes or excessive exercise. We are dedicating ourselves to a life founded on something deeper and more solid.

Whether we recite the refuges in private or whilst amongst others, we can rely on the repetition of familiar phrases as a way of deepening our relationship with the Buddha. Like narrow cart wheels scoring ridges into the hard earth, our brains form pathways that connect this verse to an experience of refuge. When we say the words we may feel empty, as if we are going through the motions, but we can trust that something is happening – just as when we say the nembutsu. The Buddha is listening, and she is ready to receive us. I take refuge in the Buddha. Namo Amitabhaya.

On being a Buddhist priest who doesn't like meditation

I am not a good meditator. I rarely look forward to sitting meditation. I don't settle very easily. I often spend the time thinking about what I'm going to do later. I don't do very much of it.

I started meditating formally when I was in my twenties, and I became interested in Suzuki Roshi's writings. I visited a local Zen centre and was very inspired by the teacher who ran it – she glowed. I liked the idea of being a Zen Buddhist very much. All you needed to do was sit zazen. It fitted my aesthetic at the time – my minimalist tendencies, my appreciation of simplicity and silence.

I used to sit for twenty minutes at a time in my tiny office which was more of a corridor, on my dark grey zafu. I would follow Suzuki Roshi's instructions – positioning my hands in the correct way, paying attention to my breath, and letting my thoughts blow through the empty room of my consciousness like dry leaves. It was always a struggle to sit regularly. I did it every morning and sometimes every evening, flexing my self-discipline muscles, but it never felt like a natural part of my day.

This morning I went upstairs for our usual half an hour of meditation in the shrine room. As I sat, my brain whirred. I spent most of my quiet time sorting through an interpersonal problem, listening to the rain and planning this chapter. It was only near the end of the session that I remembered what I was meant to be doing. Sitting with the Buddha!

I can't remember when I first realised that I could see sitting meditation as hanging out with the Buddha. I know that it was a trick I used to help me find the meditation more bearable. A meditation practice was something I felt I ought to have, and my response to this 'ought' was squirming resistance. Reframing it as sitting with the Buddha simplified the practice. It took away any expectations of having to 'do it properly', and released me to simply be there for a little while in the company of the Buddha. I didn't have to do anything – just remain quietly in his presence.

I now see this trick as being a way of reframing meditation as refuge rather than as a tool that will bring me certain benefits - calm, spiritual experiences, a new and improved identity as a good Buddhist practitioner, and ultimately enlightenment. I am a sucker for self-power practices. I love the idea of being able to pull myself up by my own bootstraps. The idea that meditation would make me a better and more spiritual person was both a blessing and a curse. As I sat, I simultaneously felt excited about finally being able to do something that would perfect me, and judged myself as not being any good at it at all.

These days I joke that I'm lucky to be a Pureland Buddhist rather than a Zen Buddhist. My primary practice is nembutsu – saying the name of Amida Buddha. This is how I now take refuge and find a settled faith. Although the great sage Honen recited many nembutsu himself, Shinran, his most famous student and founder of the largest school of Pureland Buddhism in Japan, asserted that one nembutsu said with complete trust was enough. All I need to do is say 'Namo Amida Bu'. What a relief.

I do think that sitting meditation is helpful for me. It shows me how my mind works, and it does allow the muddy water a chance to settle. I have even had spiritual experiences whilst doing zazen – I have felt suddenly deeply and tenderly connected to the Buddha, or my body has expanded and kept expanding until I was everywhere.

Spiritual experiences rarely seem to visit me when I'm meditating, though. I am more likely to connect with the Buddha when I am practising with other people and I feel sudden blooms of warmth for them. I feel bathed in the Buddha's golden glow when we do all-day nembutsu chanting. I make contact with the divine in Cathedrals or when chanting with Benedictine monks. The Dharma penetrates me when I stumble across a pair of deer on an early morning walk.

I'm not that keen on sitting meditation, and that's okay. I have found my own door onto the divine, or maybe Amida Buddha found me. I feel hugely grateful that he did. Namo Amida Bu.

Pausing to plug into the Buddha

Twenty minutes ago, I noticed a ball of anxiety in my stomach. It had been nagging at me for a while, like my cat Fatty nags me when he thinks it's time for his daily thyroid pills. We squish them into cheese to hide them, and Fatty goes mad for cheese. A couple of hours before they're due he starts making a chirruping noise which he repeats every ten minutes or so until I get up in frustration and shoo him from the room.

The anxiety in my stomach was building, and the thought arose: "Go and eat something." I wondered for a minute about what I might eat, and then had the presence of mind to pause. Was I hungry? No. What did I really need? I decided to do some chanting, one Namo Amida Bu for each of the fifty four beads of my mala. This took me about four minutes.

By the end of the four minutes, the anxiety had begun to subside a little. I realised that I had promised myself that I would do some writing this morning. It was already after eleven, and I had done all sorts of other things instead – caught up on the temple accounts, responded to some emails, started to plan a big project... The anxiety was the part of me that wanted to write, starting to panic that it wouldn't get a look in after all. 'You promised me!' it was saying. 'How can I trust you if you always do this?' I decided that I would make myself a hot drink, and return to my desk to get straight on with my writing. The urge to eat had left me.

It would have been a neat ending to this chapter if I'd sat down calmly, written for a couple of hours, and then gone out to lunch with my friend. Unfortunately, I checked my email after about ten minutes of writing. There were several emails from my husband Kaspa about something we're working on together, and so when he popped into my room a few minutes later I got tangled up in a complicated conversation. My anxiety returned and I got impatient with him for interrupting me, even though I'd invited him into my office. It was much easier to feel impatient with him than it was to feel angry at myself because I didn't let him know I was in the middle of something.

Back to the mala. I held the cool beads in my hands and felt tears come to my eyes. I am so tired of my tendency-towards-workaholism, which trips me up over and over again. It hurts. I am tired of taking my frustrations out on other people. I am tired of not being perfect yet.

This last sentence at least brings a smile to my lips. I feel amused at myself, and also softer and less self-critical. Yes, I tend to work too hard. Yes, I'm trying to shift this pattern, and yes, it's slow progress and there isn't an awful lot more I can do about it. I can either approach the workaholic part of me with blame and judgement, or I can approach it with love.

I plug in to the Buddha in various ways – by bowing towards one of the Buddha rupas in my room, by saying Namo Amida Bu, by using my mala or simply by sitting quietly with my eyes shut and imagining her there with me. I often forget to do it, but when I do remember it always eases things a little. It gives me a broader perspective, and it helps me to look at myself through her eyes rather than mine. Through her eyes, I'm not so bad after all.

So, the chapter is nearly written, and I have managed to give myself this time to write it. I have also apologised to my husband, dissolved the anxiety in my stomach, and recognised one of my old patterns for what it is. Every time I notice myself getting into a panic because of imagined work pressure, and I am able to empathise with that panicky part of me, it makes the panic less likely to occur again. The karmic seed (bija) arose, but I didn't plant it, or at least I managed to pull the seedling out before it produced too many more.

I still have twenty minutes before lunch with my friend. Rather than carry on with more work, I am going to sit quietly and read a book I have been enjoying. I feel a little bit foolish about all the fuss. The Buddha just keeps on smiling.

Taking refuge by finding teachers

Spiritual teachers are our guides through the wilderness. They are familiar with the terrain of refuge, not just in an intellectual way but by carrying their knowing in their bones. They have been soaked in their own teachers' wisdom, and they have combined this knowledge with their own experience to make it their own.

When we lean in to a spiritual teacher, we will be taken to places that we cannot visit on our own. Sometimes this happens in an instant, as when we fall in love at first sight, and sometimes it comes within the context of a relationship that is tested and developed over decades.

We need to retain our discernment when we are in relationship with any kind of teacher. Our teachers are human beings. As such, they will always have failings and blind spots. Sometimes it can be difficult to know who to trust, or which parts of someone to trust. Sometimes it is extremely difficult to work out if we're leaning into a blind spot, or if we're on the verge of discovering something important about our own dysfunction. Sometimes it is both.

The best and the most potentially dangerous part of being in a teacher student relationship is that we make ourselves vulnerable and trust that we will be shown something new. We put on a blindfold and ask to be led into the forest. Like all intimate relationships, this is scary. We need to find a balance between leaning in, and keeping our feet on the ground.

It is never okay to be exploited by a teacher for their own gratification. Sometimes it can be difficult for a teacher to know that they are doing this themselves – denial is a powerful force. Warning signs include being discouraged from critical thinking, talking to others or getting a second opinion; becoming isolated from your old life and relationships; requests for absolute loyalty to the teacher; the crossing of boundaries; and feelings of confusion or dissociation. If in doubt, step back and speak to someone you trust about what is happening in the relationship.

As foolish human beings, we do sometimes bruise or damage each other – but to allow this to prevent us from forming trusting relationships would be like never building a snowman because they melt. We don't have to take ultimate refuge in our teachers, but we can allow them to show us where refuge is. We receive something very precious. Over time, we want to pass on what we've received to others, and the cycle continues.

They say, 'When the student is ready, the teacher appears'. You don't have to find a way through the wilderness on your own.

What Gerald gave me

I had been falling in love with his strange poems all year. They described his intimate connection to trees and birds as he walked in the forests, and were peopled with his friends and acquaintances. They eluded my understanding just enough to flirt with me and call me forwards. They took me into a different world where his irascible, generous spirit showed me how to live.

Now I listened to him as he stood at the front of this modest hall in a small coastal town, reading them to us, as if we were his children. After the reading he signed books and I hung around at the back until he was free. Gerald Stern, here in the flesh. I stepped forwards.

"I just wanted to say thank you for your poems." He could see I meant it. "Are you a writer?" he asked. I nodded. He took my hands, squeezed them, and looked me straight in the eyes. I knew in that moment that I was understood. I can't even remember the words he spoke next. Was it something about my writing? Was it simply, 'keep going'?

The words weren't important. What I do remember is what happened next. I walked alone out of the hall, across the street and onto the cold beach. I sat down on the pebbles and I sobbed. The tears shook me as I looked out at the waves.

Later I tried to explain what had happened to the people I was sharing a house with during the poetry festival, but I struggled to describe the significance of the encounter. It wasn't just that I was grateful to Stern for his encouragement, or even that I particularly needed encouragement as a writer at that time. It was more that he'd transmitted something to me, through the poems and then through this short personal exchange, which I now had inside me. It was something about the necessary struggle of being a writer, and something about not being alone. This shining piece of Dharma would never leave me; it would stay as a part of me forever.

If we keep our eyes open, we find teachers everywhere. My first Buddhist teacher was a Japanese man who lived in America and who died in 1971, three years before I was born. I had heard about Suzuki Shunryu through a friend, and although (like Stern's poetry) I didn't understand all of what he wrote, I knew that I was in the presence of someone special, someone from whom I could learn something utterly new. I spent time with this book and with a very moving biography of him written by David Chadwick, and he introduced me to the magic of Buddhism. Fifteen years later and as an ordained priest in a different Buddhist tradition, I still count him as one of my most influential teachers.

I tend to fall for new teachers in an unseemly, head-over-heels way. When I am besotted with a new writer from the field of psychology or spirituality, it allows me to open up to their teachings and to their spirit in a whole-hearted way. I can filter their teachings later, taking a closer look at what I agree with and what I see differently. At the beginning, I just enjoy thinking that they're wonderful, and soak up everything that helps me to see the world in a different way. If we can keep our minds open, we will be more likely to find teachers where we least expect – the people who are engaged in huge struggles in their own lives, the people who drive us crazy, or the people who we've decided are 'not like us'.

I hope you can begin to open up to the wisdom that exists in those around us, and let it in. It is a gift to the person who is giving, and a gift to receive. We are all filtering what we receive from others through our own uniqueness, and passing it on. We are all be a part of the transmission of precious Dharma. We are all instruments waiting to channel God's peace. How wonderful.

Carrying our teachers around

It was late at night, we had just got onto an aeroplane, and we had already been travelling for a long time. One of my travel companions, with whom I have a close but complicated relationship, was going into meltdown. From previous experience, I knew that there was nothing I could do to help them, and also that they would probably find their own way out in time. I also felt a strong compulsion to take responsibility for their feelings, as I had done many times in the past. It was as if I was feeling the other person's intense distress and panic myself, but worse, because I had no control over them. It felt excruciating.

Eventually, as someone else tended to my companion, I managed to close my eyes. In that moment, to my surprise, my Buddhist teacher Dharmavidya appeared. He is a big man, and he was big in the scene that came to me – solid, immoveable. He made a kind of circle to protect me, and I leaned in.

Tears came to my eyes. I had thought that it was impossible to detach from my companion in these intense moments, and yet here I was, separate from them, even as they panicked less than a metre away from me. I could now look at them from 'over here', rather than being trapped in their body with them. I knew that this had only become possible because of the strength of my internalised Buddhist teacher, and I was hugely grateful to him.

Dharmavidya only appeared to me because I had plenty of real-life experiences of his strength and solidity. Once we have been in relationship with our teachers for a while, we no longer need to have them in front of us to benefit from their wisdom. We might not be able to guess exactly what they'd say, but we can usually imagine the look in their eyes as we tell them what's happening, or the way they'd deal with the same situation in their own lives.

We can internalise our teachers and take them with us wherever we go. My psychotherapy clients often tell me that they carry me around in this way, especially after we've been working together for some time. It works the same way with my psychotherapy supervisor, Nick, who supports me with the work I do with my clients. Over our time of working together I have got to know his way of approaching difficulties, and I have a strong sense of his unique spirit. When I have a dilemma between our sessions I am able to ask, 'how would Nick see this?' It literally gives me a second pair of eyes to look through, and often brings a fresh and helpful perspective to the situation.

Once I'd been able to detach from my travel companion, and I had given myself a chance to calm down, I was able to offer them my help in a very different way. I treated my companion as a fellow grown-up rather than as a child I was solely responsible for, and they responded better than I expected.

When you next feel out of your depth, you might want to wonder about whose experience you would like to draw on. It doesn't need to be someone you know in real life – it can be someone you know through books, or even a fictional character. Of course, the Buddha is always available too. We are never really alone.

Falling in love over and over

I fell in love with my husband nine years ago, and since then I have fallen seriously in love with at least a dozen other men and women. Here's a list of some of them. Terrance Keenan. Jean Vanier. Parker Palmer. Linda Gregg. Byron Katie. Richard Rohr. Rumi. John Paraskevopoulos. Marshall Rosenberg.

I could go on. This list consists of men and women I've met through their books and audio recordings. They are poets and psychologists, alcoholics and priests. All of them are teachers. All of them have spoken to me about the world in a new language, one I've become greedy to learn. All of them have left me changed, and grateful.

I began to notice how deeply I fell in love with these writers when my husband became irritated at me. I would read him quotes from my new paramours at every opportunity, and try to convince him that they didn't just have a few answers but all of them. I can see that when I'm in the early stages of my infatuation I might become a teensy bit annoying...

I do think, though, that this falling in love offers me something unique. It allows me to snuggle right up to new teachers and drink in their wisdom. My loyalty helps me be open to the things they say that I disagree with.

After I've read their third book, or spent several heady weeks in their company, I begin to sense their shadow side. I find myself Googling their name to see if I can find out any scandals about them. I feel disappointed that they don't mention something I find important, or when I find a small hole in their theories. I imagine that I can see their blind spots.

This disillusionment feels like a healthy part of the process. I see it as an inevitable part of falling in love – maybe we notice that our new partner never offers to pay for the coffees, or we discover that our friendly new colleague is sometimes deeply jealous of us. It's important for me to 'round out' the picture of my new loved ones in this way, as it brings me into a more realistic relationship with them. A similar process happened in real life with my own Buddhist teacher, as I discovered some of his limits and realised that it would be better to go elsewhere with particular struggles or koans. None of us, as far as I can tell so far, are Buddhas.

I have been through this disillusionment process with all of the writers I've fallen in love with, and occasionally it does do some damage to our relationship. I come out the other side with more distance between us. Mostly, though, I continue to love them just as much as before. I feel fond of their foibles as well as their strengths. I continue to learn from them. I feel hugely grateful for the wisdom they've passed on to me.

I've been in relationship with various Buddhas throughout my time as a Buddhist – mostly the historical Buddha, Shakyamuni, through the sutras and through the teachings of his followers, and Amida Buddha, who is at the heart of Pureland Buddhism. At the beginning of this year I started a new relationship with the Medicine Buddha, Bhaisajyaguru, after I bought a beautiful rupa of him whilst going through a crisis. Although I received excellent support from many colleagues and friends, the Medicine Buddha helped me with this crisis in a way that no human being had been able to.

Of course we can fall in love with objects too. New cars, gardens, a new brand of chocolate... Some things are more worthy of falling in love with than others, but I like to think that becoming infatuated with something can often bring us something good. It can pull us in closer to the world. It shows us things about ourselves that we might not see in any other way. It feels good! Maybe as we wobble along our twisty spiritual paths, we will find ourselves falling in love with more and more.

Taking refuge by acknowledging our limits

Darkness, being the absence of light, conjures the possibility of light. In this way, an experience of our own limited and fallible nature can point us towards something (somewhere) which is infinitely wise and loving. This is the territory of the alcoholic's 'rock bottom' and of the darkness before the dawn.

When we are forced to stop trying to run the show, we realise that the show runs pretty well without us. When we can lean back into the water, we discover that we are held.

The best thing about this route to refuge is that our limits surround us on all sides. We don't need to venture very far before we discover them, unless we have become very good at denial. Even strong denial eventually fractures, and we begin to see Leonard Cohen's crack where the light gets in.

Our limits become a vehicle for discovering the divine. Suddenly all of our petty addictions, our piques of jealousy and our lack of courage become signposts to what-we-are-not – entirely awake and free of selfishness. We don't have to seek out these limits – the universe will keep showing them to us throughout our life, shedding light on new layers of conceit as old habits wear off and fall away.

We can rely on the fact that we will continue to experience our limits, unless we become a Buddha in this lifetime. We can also rely on the softness and wholeness that lies behind every flaw. We can lean back into the water.

The heavy door of denial

Before the truth sets you free, it tends to make you miserable.
~ Richard Rohr

We human beings are very versatile. We don't like pain, or dukkha, and so we conjure an endless variety of ways to avoid it. These compulsive behaviours include anything that we're driven to do through a fear of the alternative, whether consciously or unconsciously, regardless of whether the behaviour is healthy or ethical, and regardless of any negative consequences further down the line. Let me share some of my favourites.

I eat too much chocolate. I fill my time by working too hard. I try to control people. I try to please people. I have spending binges. I nap in the afternoon after eating too much white bread. I spend way too much time on Facebook and checking my email. I feel superior to people. I procrastinate when I'm trying to write.

In some of these examples, like eating chocolate or procrastinating, the behaviour helps me to avoid dukkha in a relatively straightforward way. I want to cling onto the silky sweet sensation of chocolate on my tongue, and so I have another piece. I want to avoid the discomfort of sitting in front of a blank page, and so I decide to do the washing up first (and then take the rabbits some dandelion leaves, and then call my mum, and then dust the top shelf).

Our compulsive behaviours proliferate and become more complicated over time. If I learn that eating chocolate brings me comfort and distraction when I'm feeling sad or confused, then I'll reach for chocolate again when the feeling comes up. Before long I won't even notice the sadness arising – the desire for chocolate will be triggered before I've even felt the feeling. I might eat so much chocolate that I feel a bit sick, and that makes me feel bad about myself, which makes me sad, which makes me want more chocolate, which makes me put on weight, which makes me feel unattractive, which makes me sad, which makes me want more chocolate...

As the years go by we develop ever-more complicated relationships with our 'drugs of choice'. This is true whether our favourite drug is chocolate, anger, social anorexia, hoarding, self-harm, earning lots of money, being popular or any of the other million things we use to avoid dukkha.

I'm lucky in that most of my compulsive behaviours are relatively benign. I don't gamble my savings away, do great harm to my body, or cause considerable pain to my loved ones. Having said that, the negative consequences of my compulsions can be pretty severe. When I'm in a bad phase of using the internet, the very first thing I do on waking is look at Facebook on my phone. I'll then go online at ten minute intervals throughout the day, breaking off from whatever task I'm engaged in to reply to an email or to like a Facebook post. As you can imagine, this doesn't marry well with tasks that require uninterrupted concentration, like writing books. It also swallows all my spare time so I don't have any space to rest, and it leaves my brain feeling fragmented and antsy. I get irritable with anyone who pulls me away from my computer, and generally feel more needy and anxious. Oh, and it creates great rock-hard knots in my shoulders.

If all this (and more) is true, then why oh why do I carry on doing it?

Something that has been of inestimable value to me is the Twelve Step Programmes, all based on the original Twelve Step group Alcoholics Anonymous. Alcoholics Anonymous or AA came into being as a result of a meeting in 1935 between Bill W, a stockbroker, and Bob S, a surgeon. Both had been 'hopeless alcoholics' but, influenced by a spiritual group called the Oxford Group, Bill had discovered a way of getting and staying sober. Bill described his experience to Dr. Bob who was deeply affected by the encounter and who soon became sober himself, never to drink again. The two of them set about sharing their methods with other alcoholics, and AA has since helped millions of people around the world to attain sobriety.

Various groups running on the same principles as AA now help people suffering from all kinds of out-of-control compulsive behaviours – issues with food, gambling, drugs, sex addiction, co-dependency and more. Alongside the wisdom of Bill and Dr. Bob, members of the groups also benefit from the experience of alcoholics and other addicts who have successfully worked this programme for decades, and who know everything there is to know about the wily nature of addiction and how best to tackle it.

One of the things they say in AA is that alcoholism is 'a disease of denial'. Levels of denial tend to be very high in alcoholics and other addicts. They tell themselves that other people are drinking more than they are, that they don't drink until midday and so they don't have a problem, that they could stop any time, or that they're okay as long as they stick to wine and stay away from spirits. This denial continues as their spouses leave them, they get into debt, they are charged for drunk driving or their livers begin to fail. Alcoholics need to continue drinking to avoid the huge dukkha that has built up over the years, and to do this it is necessary to ignore the facts about the very high cost of their drinking and the extent to which they are out of control.

As an aside, it can drive you a little (or a lot) crazy to be close to someone who is deeply mired in addiction. The extent to which addicts skew reality, both their own direct experience and the things that other people and the world are telling them, creates an odd sort of denial aura which befuddles your own thinking. We begin to wonder if maybe they *are* more in control of their drinking than their friends are, and maybe it *was* just bad luck that they got caught driving when they were slightly over the limit. It can take years for the truth to catch up with both the alcoholic and with those they are in close relationship with. This is why programmes such as Al Anon which support people who are in relationships with alcoholics are so important.

In my own case, when I'm checking my email too often I downplay the effect it has on my life. Other people check their email all day long, don't they? I'm still getting my work done, aren't I? Maybe I'll stop checking so often tomorrow. I like doing it this way – have you got a problem with that? It's only when I make myself thoroughly sick, like when I've spent a desolate hour scrolling on Facebook, or avoided writing for a whole day, that I catch glimpses of the truth and consider trying to change my habits (again). Sometimes this clear-seeing persists, and sometimes it falls away again as I forget how sick I felt earlier and start checking email again.

How can we break through this denial? The first of the Twelve Steps is the point at which we finally acknowledge the depth of our predicament: 'I admitted I was powerless over alcohol, and that my life had become unmanageable'. For the word alcohol you can substitute your drug/s of choice – food, sex, people, overwork etc. This is the most difficult step to take, and one of the reasons why so many people don't seek help and find recovery. We wake up with another horrible hangover and slide straight back into minimising the problem or finding some other way of justifying our favourite compulsive behaviour.

Luckily, the universe has a habit of continuing to show us the things that aren't working in our lives. We come to acknowledge the extent of our denial in different ways. Sometimes one more negative consequence of our behaviour becomes the straw that broke the camel's back, like our spouse leaving us or the addiction affecting our health. Sometimes we try to cut down or give up one more time, and have a strong experience of the futility of our efforts. Sometimes we are inspired by someone who has overcome similar problems and seems to be living a free and happy life.

Whatever happens, we finally crack through our denial and admit that we are completely powerless over our compulsive behaviour. This is known as our 'rock bottom', and unfortunately some people don't reach this point before their addiction kills them. In this moment of complete honesty and desperation, we finally open the door to being helped by something (anything) other than ourselves. In the programme they call this our 'Higher Power'. Different people have different conceptions of their Higher Power – the benign unfolding of the universe, nature, the Buddha, the wisdom of the group or God. It doesn't matter what it is, it's just crucial that it isn't me, and that I'm willing to be helped by it. Over time, through listening to others and through our own experiences, we begin to develop the beginnings of trust in this Higher Power. Hope returns. Even when we only open the heavy door of denial a teensy weensy crack, there is space for a few beams of light. Through this true encounter with our limits, we turn away from ourselves and towards outside help. This is the beginning of true refuge, as Dharmavidya says in 'Questions in the Sand' below:

"The emphasis, when one takes refuge in Amida, is upon acknowledgement that the being who seeks refuge needs to do so because of being a "foolish being of wayward passion", a vulnerable, limited, deluded, error-prone mortal. Here, therefore, there is a recognition that we each manifest greed, hate, pride, worry, sloth, and a wide variety of forms of self-centredness and that, although we might improve in some areas, the fundamental propensity to give rise to such characteristics is indelible and we are, therefore, incapable of achieving our own salvation by our own self-directed efforts. This recognition adds extra power and urgency to the urge to take refuge. Taking refuge comes to have the sense of turning to a salvific power that we ourselves lack. In this act of taking refuge, therefore, there is a profound sense of letting go and of relief. We see the self-perfection project to lie in ruin, but we also feel a great gratitude for the presence and support of the Buddha who sees us in our actual state and loves us just so, even as we are. This is deeply moving."

If I can see my compulsions as an inevitable part of being a bombu human, they become a door into a relationship with the divine. I can melt into refuge, and allow the Buddhas to support me. Sometimes this might help to release me from my addictions, and sometimes it won't. Amida accepts me either way, and I am safe in his arms.

The seductive deliciousness of praise

This morning I noticed a new online review of our book, 'Just As You Are'. It was our thirteenth five star review. I felt a familiar rush of warm excitement – ooh, someone has been impressed by what we wrote! They liked it enough to give it five out of five stars!

Receiving praise is so delicious.

The feeling faded, and I wanted more. I clicked to see the other reviews this person had written, interested in what else she had read. I was hoping she read scholarly Buddhist tomes, of course, and that she had given them two or three stars each at most. Instead I saw that she read a wide range of fiction and spiritual writing, some of it of dubious quality, and that she had given raving five star reviews to all but a couple of the scores she'd read. I smiled wryly as the warm feeling started to fade...

Yesterday I was speaking to my psychotherapy supervisor about a book where the well-known author speaks about how fleeting and empty the pleasures of fame are. Logically, I know this to be true. I have had some experience of being famous and receiving praise. When my fourth novel sold very well and I watched it rise ever upwards in the charts, I felt like I was on drugs. I found myself needing a higher and higher chart position to maintain my own high. I became greedy for more and more glowing reviews. The sales peaked and eventually came down, as all things must do, and I was left with a huge praise hangover. I didn't get to 'keep' any of the self-esteem I thought I was receiving from those readers. The praise went into my huge hungry ghost belly and left me as starving as ever.

The Buddha repeatedly warns us of the dangers of falling for praise and blame. I like how he puts it here in the Muni Sutta (SN 1:12, translated by Thanissaro Bhikkhu) which describes the qualities of a perfect sage:

> The wandering solitary sage,
> uncomplacent, unshaken by praise or blame.
> Unstartled,   like a lion at sounds.
> Unsnared,   like the wind in a net.
> Unsmeared,   like a lotus in water.
> Leader of others, by others unled:
> The enlightened call him a sage.

So is it best to close our eyes and ears to praise and blame completely? My supervisor suggested yesterday that it's okay for us to enjoy the feelings we get from praise, as long as we don't get tangled up and start clinging. This would be like receiving an exquisite macadamia-praline chocolate from someone and enjoying every morsel, without feeling like we need to find a way (at any cost) of getting a second or a third. We accept the chocolate we are given, we savour it, and then we move on.

When I read the new review I enjoyed it, but then I got my feet stuck in the sticky sweetness. What kind of person was giving me this praise? How discerning were they? How much credit could I give myself for those five stars? I led myself up the garden path and, to mix my metaphors, headed straight into a blind alley.

The next time I receive praise, whether it's someone liking my new haircut or an excellent review from an esteemed peer, I will aim to be unshaken by it. I will enjoy the taste of it, acknowledging the mix of truth and fiction it will inevitably contain, and then allow it to pass from my sight as I keep walking. Unstartled, like a lion at sounds. Alternatively, in the Pureland Buddhist version, I will get my feet stuck in the praise again and fall flat on my face, knowing that Amida Buddha loves me just the same. Either way, I will give myself permission to enjoy the warmth on my face as the sun of praise comes out from behind a cloud.

Dealing with jealousy

This morning our copy of Tricycle arrived – the Buddhist equivalent of Vogue. In it are glossy photos of Buddhas and mandalas, adverts for zafus and malas, and lots of names of famous Dharma teachers – doing talks, writing books, and generally being inspirational and awesome.

This magazine often invites my jealousy out to play. I flip between feeling outraged that I'm not already in the magazine myself (with a regular three page feature), to feeling despair about the appropriately miniscule size of my influence and the audacity of ever wishing for anything more.

After putting the magazine down and coming down to earth, I remembered that I actually already have been in Tricycle, with an extract from the book I wrote with my husband. This is the trouble with jealousy and a lust for fame – seeking relief through receiving affirmation is like trying to quench our thirst with sand.

We can guess how the Buddha felt about fame. In 8:6 of the Anguttara Nikaya (translated by Bhikkhu Bodhi) he says:

"Bhikkhus, these eight worldly conditions revolve around the world, and the world revolves around these eight worldly conditions. What eight? Gain and loss, disrepute and fame, blame and praise, and pleasure and pain.

Gain obsesses his mind, and loss obsesses his mind. Fame obsesses his mind, and disrepute obsesses his mind. Blame obsesses his mind, and praise obsesses his mind. Pleasure obsesses his mind, and pain obsesses his mind. He is attracted to gain and repelled by loss. He is attracted to fame and repelled by disrepute. He is attracted to praise and repelled by blame. He is attracted to pleasure and repelled by pain. Thus involved with attraction and repulsion, he is not freed from birth, from old age and death, from sorrow, lamentation, pain, dejection, and anguish; he is not freed from suffering, I say."

We know it's not helpful to have feelings such as jealousy, but unfortunately most of us are not Buddhas yet. What might actually help us with the feelings of wanting more or comparing ourselves to other people when they do inevitably arise? Here's what helps me.

Recently I have been looking at my contribution to the 'Buddhist world' in the same way as I look at my contribution in our little temple. I make myself available to help in whatever way is necessary. Sometimes this is leading a service, and representing the Dharma at the front of a shrine room full of people. Sometimes this is cleaning the toilets, or picking flowers for a guest room, or doing the accounts.

In an ideal world, I will perform each of these tasks with the same levels of care and attention, and know that they are all offerings to the Buddha, regardless of whether other people notice them or how much praise I receive.

I'm trying to see my job in the bigger Buddhist world in the same way. I'll keep writing articles and books to the best of my ability, and sending them out into the ether. Sometimes lots of people will read them and enjoy them, and sometimes not. That's okay.

What also helps me when jealousy arrives is not to castigate myself, but to have empathy towards the parts of me that feel overlooked, or overworked, or lonely. The jealousy is pointing to something inside me that needs attention – and this won't be achieved by just ignoring it, but instead by asking the Buddha to shine his golden light on it and soaking it in.

When the jealousy fades, I feel differently. I can discern between those teachings in the magazine I find helpful and those I don't, receive inspiration from what I've read, and enjoy knowing that there are so many people out there in the world, spreading the good seeds of the Dharma. I can also feel grateful that I'm not a big name in the Buddhist world, which I am sure brings its own heavy responsibilities and complications.

The Zen teacher Shozan Jack Haubner puts this beautifully: "My job as a middle-aged middle manager of the middle way is the same as that of any lay practitioner, right on up to the most enlightened being on earth: we must all commit wholeheartedly, moment after moment, to the life we have, instead of fantasizing about a different life while putting down or envying those who are supposedly living it. When I start feeling jealous of others, it's a warning sign that I've become a little bit too entranced by some idea of myself and have lost touch with the reality of my life. Someone else seems to better represent this idea of myself than I do, and suddenly I want his life instead of my own. Zen practice, however, teaches you to completely be yourself – if you don't, who will?"

I am grateful for the life I have. It has pros and cons, just as everyone's life does, and I could always 'do better'. I'm working with the karma I was handed, and I'm enjoying myself as much as I can. I'm living Satya's life. It's pretty awesome.

Taking refuge by seeing clearly

If we can see with the eyes of the Buddha, everything around us becomes a signpost to the Pure Land.

We watch a squirrel teetering across an overhead power line, and see the fragility and preciousness of life. We see people being cruel, and understand the depth of the suffering that has led them to their actions. We lift our mug to our lips, and marvel at the myriad of activities and circumstances that were necessary to bring us this gift of fragrant tea. We are grateful.

We usually wear me-glasses, which obscure the Buddha's clear vision. We see everything as a function of ourselves, wondering what use it might be to us. We objectify people, places and things.

When we take off our me-glasses, our partner is no longer a layabout who hasn't done the washing up but someone who is feeling anxious about tomorrow's hospital visit and is distracting himself with television. The temple rabbit Joe isn't a grumpy so-and-so who refuses to be stroked but a curious, alert, wondrous being with his own preferences and beautiful floppy ears.

How do we take these glasses off? First of all we need to notice that we are wearing them. We begin to notice how everything around us is a signpost back to our own ego. We become curious about how it is to be that rabbit, or that plant. We allow what is outside of us to present itself to us, without interfering. We wait, watch and wonder.

Taking refuge helps us to see more clearly, as refuge reduces the need we have to prop ourselves up or defend our ego. Seeing more clearly helps us to take refuge, as we are affected by the wholeness of what we see. Everything is shining.

Choosing chocolates and missing out

I am somewhat of a chocolate connoisseur, and so when I find companies that make high quality vegan chocolates I get very excited. Bianca Marton is one of those companies. They also happen to make delicious caramel chocolates, which are rare in the vegan world.

I had treated myself to an exquisite box of their handmade chocolates a few times, containing a random selection of their chocolates. The last time I ordered myself a small box, I wrote in the instructions that I needed the chocolates to be vegan and alcohol free and that I also really liked the caramel ones. I also ordered another little box of six caramel chocolates, just to be on the safe side.

When the box arrived, I opened it and was disappointed to find that it was almost entirely full of caramel chocolates, just as I had asked for. I suddenly missed the passion fruit chocolate from last time, and the rose and violet creams. I missed the one flavoured with real coffee. I missed the surprises.

I understand why I wrote the note. I'd enjoyed the single caramel chocolate in my last box so much, I'd wanted to completely control my experience of the next box. I'd wanted to cling on to that pleasure and intensify it. I'd wanted to avoid the slightly less enjoyable orange chocolate. Buddhism tells us that this is what we do – we pull what we enjoy towards us, and we push unpleasant things away. We behave as if it is possible to manipulate the world to suit us. We don't only want to keep the bad stuff away, but we want more and more of the good stuff –

ten caramel chocolates, fifty. If only we could get the instructions right, and if only we could get everyone to listen to us properly and obey...

My attempt at complete control of my chocolate-eating pleasure led me to an impoverished experience. When we are too specific about what we want, this is what happens. We can see this playing out in other mundane examples – when we have a specific pair of trousers in mind when we go shopping, and so miss the ones that would look equally good on us – or in major ways, as when our list of requirements for a future partner excludes all human beings.

I am more able to enjoy the world-as-it-is when I feel less anxious. I am more able to deal with surprises, and be flexible with my plans. I trust that I will be looked after. When friends cancel I think, "oh, that gives me a chance to read my new novel," rather than, "maybe she hates me". When a colleague gets the praise I was hoping for, I can feel pleased for them and trust that my work has value too.

What helps me to feel less anxious is taking refuge in Amida Buddha. I have a place to rest where I don't have to worry about how much good stuff I'm going to get. I don't have to defend myself against all the difficult things that will undoubtedly happen, today or tomorrow or next week. I know that I will be okay, even when I'm not okay. I am reminded that I am not at the centre of the universe, and knowing this makes life more fun, not less. I remember the pleasures of giving, and the satisfactions of emptiness as well as fullness.

I can even be grateful for boxes full of creamy, delicious caramel chocolates.

On suffering

*Everything in your life is there as a vehicle for your transformation.
Use it! ~ Ram Dass*

Suffering is where the Buddha began. The first of his four noble
truths is that, as an inevitable part of life, we will encounter
suffering. The word that he originally used, dukkha, has been
translated in various ways – most commonly as suffering, but
also as 'unsatisfactoriness', 'dissatisfaction', or 'pervasive disease'.

Let's see how it works. Right now I am sitting at my desk
in my little office. I'm in an alcove – to my right a golden
Buddha is sitting on my bookcase, haloed by the deep blue wall.
To my left are the two grey chairs where I sit with my therapy
clients, and between here and the chairs is a window which
looks out onto the garden.

When I look out I can see the blue bench. Aha – here is
my first small experience of dukkha. The bench is currently lit
up by sunlight. I'm tempted. I know that if I accepted the sun's
invitation I would receive an expansive view of the valley
stretching out behind our sloped gardens. I would see the wide
sky dappled with cloud, and the spire of Malvern Priory. I would
feel the late September sun warming my face... Instead of all
that I'm stuck inside, wrestling with words.

Okay, I'll bring my focus back to my work again. And
now I feel thirsty. I go and make myself a hot drink. A white
mug of dark chicory, frothy on top. Too hot! I'll wait a bit. Still a
bit too hot. Another minute... Ah, yes, that's nice. And then I get

lost in my writing and I forget it, so the next sip is too cold. A twinge in my back – change position, and it goes. Now there's a lock of hair tickling my cheek. I tuck it behind one ear. Someone is making a distracting noise outside. I look. Oh, there's that blue bench again. And now the phone rings. I jump from my desk and run to answer it. An automated voice: This is an important call about your boiler... Junk call!

These cycles of dissatisfaction and resolution play out on a larger scale, too. Our close relationships all involve loss – both the big final loss of death, abandonment or failure, and smaller losses along the way, when our friends and family either knowingly or unknowingly let us down. There's no experience of love without disappointment. Our bodies are unpredictable and, if we're lucky enough to live into old age, they become increasingly unreliable and saddled with pain. Sometimes we manage to hold onto the things we want and push away the things we don't want, but only for a little while. Here's how the Buddha put it:

"Birth is dukkha, aging is dukkha, death is dukkha; sorrow, lamentation, pain, grief, and despair are dukkha; association with the unbeloved is dukkha; separation from the loved is dukkha; not getting what is wanted is dukkha." (SN 56.11)

Dukkha is the first of the four noble truths, with the implication that it is a good place to begin. Why is it important to face dukkha in this way? The first is that it's always good to remember that we are not alone. In my job as a therapist, my clients tell me things that they've never told another soul. They are sometimes surprised when I listen calmly and let them know that I get it. They discover that their truths aren't so horrifying after all. However deeply you are suffering, and whatever drastic measures you have taken to try and avoid this suffering, you are not the only one. We all suffer, even those of us who give a pretty good impression to the contrary, and all of humanity has this in common.

The second reason to face dukkha is that it helps us to see reality more clearly and completely, and this is always a good thing. We get into trouble when we try to massage the truth. Whether our dishonesty is uncovered or not, this hiding of the truth takes energy to maintain and leads to an unnecessary extra layer of suffering. We are all in denial about all kinds of things, minor and major. The more we can move towards being honest with ourselves and others, the freer we become. Dharma can be seen as the absolute truth of all things, and as we come into relationship with these things-as-they-are, we are changed by them. Dukkha is a part of this truth.

Thirdly, as Ram Dass reminds us in the quote at the start of this chapter, dukkha can point us towards the light. Whenever we suffer, we are being shown that we are attached to a particular outcome. This points to a choice between clinging and suffering, or letting go and resting in faith. Letting go of attachment doesn't mean that bad things will stop happening to us or that we will live happily ever after. Dukkha is still the first noble truth. The Buddha still made mistakes after he was enlightened, coped with squabbling in the Sangha, endured periods of sickness, and died. Meeting things-as-they-are simply means experiencing whatever is happening without adding another layer of suffering. Oh, I notice that I want to go and sit on the blue bench. Oh, I notice that I'm repelled by the coldness of this drink. Oh, I'm grieving, and it really hurts. As Dharmavidya puts it, 'I'm not okay, and you're not okay, and that's okay'.

Finally, being honest about the suffering in the world can also nudge us to appreciate the sweetness of life. It's so easy to take the good things for granted. I am reminded of how wonderful it is to breathe easily when I'm coming to the other side of a bad cold, or how good it is to have enough to eat when I'm starving hungry. We can also notice the suffering of others and allow this to point us to gratitude for our own circumstances.

This chapter is finished, and so now I'm going to put the kettle on and take a fresh mug of chicory out with me to that blue bench. Maybe the sun will go in before I get to it, and maybe it won't. I'll appreciate the view either way.

Crack cocaine for bunnies

I want to introduce you to Poppet and Peter, the temple bunnies. I call them Pops and Peetle. Peetle has cataracts and is practically blind. Pops had one of her back legs amputated last year after an accident.

They don't let this hold them back. They live outside, in a hutch inside an aviary, so they have their own front lawn. Once a day we let them out into the temple garden so they can have a longer run. Peetle finds his way around just fine, only running into things when a loud noise startles him. Three-legged Pops still runs much faster than I can catch her, and when they have a digging project on, she's like a blur of burrowing as she disappears into the earth.

They love each other very much. They spend their days together, and when they are feeling extra soppy they will snuggle their heads underneath each other, asking to have their ears licked.

They love each other very much, that is, until I take them an occasional carrot. As soon as I snap it in two their noses prick up and they run over. They snatch their half from me and peg it to opposite ends of the hutch, guarding it jealously as they eat. If Pops gets distracted by Peetle's carrot and misses the one I'm offering her, she chases him round and round and round. And round. And round. Carrots are crack cocaine for bunnies. They do NOT want to share.

This is how it is for us too. When we get our own 'carrots', we forget that we love each other. After cooking dinner for our friend I remember that I have some special posh chocolates in the top drawer, and find myself offering them a cheaper chocolate mint instead. Posh chocolates are my carrots. I also feel carroty when I want things to be done in a very particular way, when I feel poor and cling onto my money, when I'm enjoying talking about myself... What are your carrots?

The Buddha told us that we get into trouble when we start clinging to our carrots. When we are promised a nice carrot, or when someone tries to take our carrot away, or when our friend is enjoying a big juicy carrot right next to us, feelings will come up.

The feelings are inevitable, but we do have some control over what we do next. We can either act on our jealousy, or transmute it into mudita (joy for another's happiness). We can hoard our carrots, or we can gently practice giving a portion of them away. This is the third noble truth, where the Buddha told us to build an 'earth bank' around the fire of our reactions and feelings. He asked us to use this energy to take the noble path, as a way of fuelling us into taking right action. It's not always easy.

Pureland Buddhism adds that we will inevitably be driven crazy by carrots until the day we die. That's okay – Amida accepts our carroty natures, and invites us to take refuge in his arms. Cloaked in his love, we can go back out into the world and try again (and again) to share our carrots.

Pops and Peetle still love each other, even when they are trying to steal each other's carrots. Their love is momentarily eclipsed by the carrot-lust, like the sun behind clouds. This is helpful to remember – especially if we are feeling upset by someone who is trying to steal our carrot. When we say 'if they really loved me, they wouldn't...' – we are often underestimating the power of their carrot-lust. Maybe they'll find a way of kicking the habit, of building their own earth bank, and maybe they won't. We may need to let go of waiting for them to change, and focus instead on how we can be okay with them as they are. Whatever we decide, we can trust that they do care about us, behind all that compulsion or meanness or selfishness.

Carrots are everywhere. And the sun never stops shining – not for a single second.

Taking refuge by turning to something Other

Connecting with the Other takes us outside of our small selves.

What is the Other? Anything that isn't me. It might be the swifts swooping and arcing outside my window. It might be that wisp of cloud far above. It might be the resonant music of the plumbing as water bangs in the pipes.

Every time we allow ourselves to be influenced by the Other, the tight circle of our preoccupations is drawn a little larger. We understand something that we were unable to understand before, from within the constraints of our previous knowledge. The curtains are drawn aside and a new corner lights up.

We can try to see more clearly from our end, but being influenced by the Other is more a matter of letting go. I don't need to try and seek it out. I just allow that huge tree outside my window to step forwards, with its leaves moving like the fur of a huge creature, riffling in the wind. The Other is already here and, when we let it, it shows us something. Right now it is reminding me of how small I am, and of how I don't need to worry quite so much about anything.

For Pureland Buddhists, the five most powerful Others are the five jewels; Amitabha, the Buddha, the Dharma, the Sangha and the Pure Land. Becoming conscious of these things both in our ordinary lives and in the hazy mystery of our imaginations and dreams helps us find a true refuge.

As we loosen our hold on our favourite preoccupations, we begin to hear the music which was there all along. We notice patterns and signs. We receive help. The Other steps in when we let it, and it always knows more than we do. It wants to show us something, and it will – as soon as we are ready to open ourselves up.

On paying attention

Proper attention is our refuge now, our perch and our praise.
~ Charles Wright

In my mouth there is the echo of mint tea. Outside I can see crumpled Japanese anemone leaves nodding in the breeze, and the weight of a brick keeping some black weed-suppressing fabric flat. I light a short stick of incense and watch a line of grey cloud curl from the tip. My fingers smell of woodsmoke.

There is a way of paying attention that brings us closer to the Other, to the world-as-it-is. It is always available to us, however many senses we have intact. We could spend a whole day paying attention to the sounds that enter us. When we slow down and tune in to what is present, something miraculous happens – we come home to our bodies, and we come home to the world. Beauty appears.

Why is this? You could describe this kind of paying attention as a mindfulness practice, in which we bring our attention continuously and without judgement to the present moment. This is a practice that is currently very in vogue. Practising mindfulness is a good thing. Amongst other things it can help our over-busy minds to settle, allow us to see things more clearly, and help us to face strong emotion rather than being swept away by it.

As a Pureland Buddhist, I also see paying attention as a form of nembutsu. Nembutsu is the spiritual practice at the heart of our form of Buddhism. We practice nembutsu when we say the name of Amida Buddha, the Buddha of Infinite Light.

When we do this – *Namo Amida Bu* – we are forming a connection with Amida Buddha and all of her wisdom, patience, courage and love. We are turning towards the light.

In this moment of refuge, we are taken outside of our small minds and are plugged into something bigger. Our egos, with all their wheedling and restlessness, are comforted and silenced. Oh, look at the tip of that candle flame swaying as if it is hearing music! Oh, listen to the animal growl sounds my stomach is making! Oh, see the complexity of the shadow shapes in that single crumpled tissue! Oh, oh, oh!

Paying attention connects us to awe. It reminds us that the universe is much bigger and more complicated than we can ever know. Whether or not we can feel the love of Amida Buddha, we can receive the intricate design of that spray of cow parsley, or the gift of cool earth on the soles of our feet. We are so small, and we have received so much. Even the mud and the thorns and a rabbit's broken leg have something to teach us.

A caveat: it is not helpful to become so in love with the present moment that we neglect all else. Our memories anchor us. Our ability to look forward into the future and to make plans allows us to achieve good and necessary things. Sometimes 'present momentism' is used as a way of avoiding what needs to be faced – difficult emotions, or actions we'd rather not take. If you find yourself repeatedly dragging yourself into the present moment, don't forget to be curious about what you might be hiding from.

So how can you get a taste of this form of nembutsu? Anything that pulls you into relationship with the Other will do the trick. Say 'Namo Amida Bu' as often as you remember, out loud or in your head, even if you're not quite sure what you're saying or why. Take a photo every day, or write a *small stone* – a short piece of writing that describes a fully-engaged moment. Spend five minutes sitting quietly and paying attention to what's going on in your body.

Plug yourself in to the mains, and keep yourself charged up. Namo Amida Bu.

Sparks of joy

Last month we cleared out ten huge bags of clothing and three full car-loads of recycling and rubbish from our flat.

We don't have a big flat – we live on the ground floor of the temple and have a tiny bathroom, my little office, an open space for our living room and kitchen, and a small bedroom. We don't really have a lot of stuff. So where did it all come from?

The week before, my friend had leant me her copy of Marie Kondo's 'The Life-Changing Magic of Tidying'. It was the kind of book I find delicious and I devoured it quickly – learning about Kondo's many years of experience of tidying, and making sense of her method.

I roped in Kaspa, and as the book suggests we began by gathering all the items of clothing we owned and putting them into piles on the living room carpet. Our coats, our smart clothes which live in a different cupboard, our pyjamas, drawerfuls of socks – the lot. There was a very big pile! The next phase was to become quiet and pick up the items one by one, holding them close to our hearts. Did whatever I was holding spark joy in me? If so, it goes into the 'keep' pile. If not, we thank it for its service and then recycle it.

The process was fascinatingly unpredictable. I was surprised at the lack of spark when I picked up a favourite pair of trousers. On reflection, they were too big for me since I'd lost weight. They went into the recycling. I picked up a paint-stained jersey top, expecting to have to throw it away. No – the warm feeling was immediate. Keep, for wearing whilst painting. I thought I liked those socks – but no joy. Ah, on further

148

inspection, there's a big hole in them. I've kept this intricately embroidered peacock jacket for 20 years, never wearing it, and even though I love it there's no joy and I feel sadness as I put it onto the pile of items to give away as presents.

The other surprise was how emotional the process was. I felt sad as I let go of sentimental items from my past, thanking the objects for their service, and letting go of that period of my life. I felt disappointed in myself as I let go of clothes I always thought I would wear one day, finally admitting that I'm not the kind of person to make use of a glamorous sparkly skirt or a skimpy sun dress. I was shedding layers – versions of myself that I had been attached to, but that were no longer (or had never been) true.

This process is entirely other-centred. Rather than imagining that we know what's best for us, instead we are asking the objects around us for their wisdom. Our clothes told us whether they wanted to stay with us or to go somewhere new, whether to be sold in a charity shop, given to friends or burnt into ashes which will nourish the earth. Somehow they knew better than we did.

Kondo speaks a lot in the book about treating our objects kindly – not stacking items so the ones on the bottom get squashed, and saying thank you to them once they've done their job. I was moved to read that before she begins the decluttering process in a new client's household she performs a little ritual, prostrating in silence and asking the house for its help. As I write this chapter I am experiencing a new appreciation for the objects I'm using right now – the intricacy of the keyboard which is producing these words, the desk lamp which is providing me with light, and the beautiful wood of my desk which grew goodness knows where.

By the end of our clothes-sorting day our wardrobes and drawers had been drastically slimmed down. When I replace clothes now I don't have to cram another hanger onto the rail, or shove a jumper into an already-full drawer. Each item of clothing has room to breathe. In the weeks following I've needed to buy myself a couple of second hand jumpers and a new dressing gown (I'd bought the threadbare gown I'd been wearing when I was thirteen) but apart from that I had plenty of clothes. Now I always wear the clothes that bring me joy – I don't have a choice. I look smarter, as if I care about myself more. I also look more like a 'current' version of myself. Later we moved on to sort the huge cupboard in our hallway, the boiler room, our books, the two drawers of 'chaos' and more. As each area was completed we felt tired but satisfied – cleansed and holy.

If we can tune in to the wisdom of the things around us, they won't just help us with de-cluttering. Asking objects for their advice can make space in our ego and allow something new to enter us. When opening our fridge to make lunch we can ask what wants to be used up, rather than following our preferences. When painting a picture, we can ask the paintbrush what colour it wants next.

Of course the ultimate Other for Pureland Buddhists is Amida Buddha, who we can also enter into conversation with. We can ask him for advice, and then wait patiently to see what solutions might unfold around us. We can ask him to take away our compulsions and our bad habits. We can bow before him, making ourselves smaller, allowing ourselves to be helped and loved.

When we remember the sacredness of all objects, we live with more gratitude (thank you, cup, for carrying my tea) and more kindness (thanks for your support, shoes, I'll put you neatly on the shoe rack where you like to live rather than shoving you into that cupboard). We will receive their wisdom. We will find a way to live in harmony with all the objects that share our house and our lives with us. Most of all, we will have an experience of living a sacred life, with everything, including us, playing their own parts with modesty and with grace.

What the rabbits taught me

When a new templemate moved in last year, she brought her two rabbits with her. I hadn't spent any time with rabbits before, and during the summer I started getting to know them. I lay on the grass in the sunshine next to their run, and watched them as they went about their lives. Poppet, the white and tan female, was definitely in charge. Peter, the big black one, lived at a slower pace and had cataracts which meant he was nearly blind. After a few months their owner made a decision to rehome them, and by this time I had fallen thoroughly in love with them. They became temple bunnies.

To begin with I didn't know how to be around them. We've always had cats, and I know where I am with cats. If you make 'hello' noises as you approach a cat, proffering a tentative hand, they will often come to you. Poppet and Peter didn't come to me. They hated being picked up with a hind-leg kicking passion. They tolerated being stroked but didn't seem too bothered either way. Without these ways of connecting, how could we have any kind of relationship?

I watched them. I realised that when they put their ears at a certain angle it meant they were nervous. I saw Poppet bow her forehead towards Peter so he could groom her. I read online that when they thumped their back feet they were warning other rabbits of danger – the shape of a bird overhead, or the smell of a dog.

I sat with them. I spent time in their new rabbit enclosure with them, a 12 foot aviary with their hutch at one end. I watched them do binkies, where they leap in the air with joy and kick their legs together. I noticed them gradually getting more comfortable in my company, and smiled as they suddenly threw themselves onto their backs in the sunshine, their eyes half closed, a blissful surrendering.

I talked to them. I told them about my day, and I grumbled at them when they didn't want to go back into their enclosure after their exercise in the top garden. I told them how beautiful they were.

I cared for them. We found out that if we didn't spay Poppet she'd have an eighty percent chance of getting uterine cancer by the age of three (domestic rabbits can live to twelve years). We learnt what diet they needed, and discovered more and more things that they found delicious – dandelion leaves, sprigs of hazel branches, the leafy stalks around cauliflowers. We built them their luxury aviary accommodation and changed their litter tray every day. They were happy bunnies.

A month ago, I went into the aviary with Felix (aged three) to discover that Poppet had badly broken her leg. The bone was snapped and visible. He ran for help and I took her into my arms. She didn't struggle. We drove to the emergency vet, and as I cupped her close to me I prayed that she wouldn't die of shock. Her breathing changed and I thought we were going to lose her. We chanted as we drove, in between arguing about getting lost – Namo Quan Shi Yin Bosat, calling on the Bodhisattva of Compassion and asking her to come to Poppet's aid.

She survived the journey, and the next day our vet amputated her back left leg. After a couple of weeks in a run in our living room, kept company by Peter, she went back outside.

With some adjustments (carpet in her hutch so she doesn't slip over, keeping an eye on the ear she can no longer keep clean) she is doing fabulously. I tried to catch her the other day and I wasn't quick enough. Our tripod bunny.

The rabbits have reminded me how scary it is to have complete responsibility for another living thing. If we don't fill up their water bottle, they don't drink. They have also taught me something about how it is to love without conditions. They don't jump on my lap. They don't purr. Peter seems quite pleased to be stroked these days, but he still won't come towards my hand (unless I'm holding something tasty!).

I love them and I want them to enjoy their lives. What makes me happy is making them happy. It is enough. They have shown me this, and I am grateful.

What happens when we take refuge?

Once we start practising taking refuge, what happens to us? Does life become simple and pleasurable? Do the flaws in our character get completely ironed out? Do we stop being frightened or disappointed or angry or jealous or sad?

Yes and no. Refuge does help us with these things, and life does become easier. The Buddha also told us that there is no avoiding dukkha – even once we're enlightened. When we encounter dukkha, energy arises, and the Buddha encouraged us to use this energy to do good.

Taking refuge helps us to get better at spotting this reaction-energy or fire when it arises, and at catching it before it burns out of control. It also helps us to bear the heat of dukkha without feeling overwhelmed, disheartened or obliterated.

Taking refuge is the best antidote to fear I know. This section of the book looks at some of the side effects of a reduction in fear. We receive healing and happiness, we get better at being kind, we blame less, we get better at handling change and difficulty, we create Pure Lands, and we enjoy the deliciousness of surrender.

You'll have your own side effects to add to the list. Try it, and watch your life slowly change.

With refuge we heal

We all hold wounds from our past. Sometimes these wounds accumulate, and our grief or anger or feelings of powerlessness threaten to burst out and drown us. Our system keeps things ticking along – by repressing feelings, using denial and blame, falling into addictions, distracting ourselves with relationships, and in many other ways.

When our system is under strain and afraid that it might shatter, it freezes instead.

In order to heal, we need to feel safe enough to let our system fall apart before it finds a way to put itself back together again. Sometimes we find ourselves overwhelmed with depression or confusion as soon as we are through a bad patch and our lives improve – this is why. Our system needs to know that the risk of dealing with the backlog is worth taking, and that this uncomfortable reorganisation isn't likely to throw us into madness or suicide.

When our new rabbits Smokey and Joe first met our current rabbit, Poppet, they fought viciously. We doubted that they would ever find a way of getting along. We were told to make their cage smaller and, counterintuitive though it was, we did it.

In this smaller cage, they almost immediately settled down. The bonding proceeded with less fighting, and before too long they were grooming each other and sleeping alongside each other. The walls held them tighter, and the conflict worked itself out.

Refuge offers us a safe space where we can begin to heal. Sometimes this makes us feels worse before we feel better, like a spot that has to grow before it bursts.

We can trust the process. We can let it unfold, and rest in refuge. We can witness our healing, and appreciate our beautiful scars.

Help from the Medicine Buddha

Kaspa and I were stood at our Buddhist stall at a Wellbeing Fair in the centre of Malvern, offering leaflets and books for sale. A well-dressed, older woman was one of the first people to approach us that day. Her husband stood back, looking slightly sheepish. She told us that it was her husband who'd encouraged her to talk to us, as the first time she had just walked past. Then she said, "When I first heard the Buddhists were coming to Malvern, I was horrified."

What she said sent me into shock. I knew I'd heard her correctly but I asked her to repeat it, partly because I wanted to see if she would hear herself and realise she'd used a word that was too strong. "Horrified?" "Yes, horrified." She was just as emphatic and her tone was pleasant but there was also a tight, fierce anger. "I couldn't believe it would happen in Malvern." When I found my tongue again, I went on automatic and tried to get her to like me. I put on my best ingratiating smile and empathised with her. After the couple had gone I repeated the story of what had happened to six or seven people I knew, expressing how stunned it had left me.

Later that evening, after a full and nourishing day of lovely conversations with people at the Fair, I found myself struggling with horrible indigestion. I limped around the house, trying to find a way to get comfortable, and finally found myself in my office with my new Medicine Buddha.

I had found this unusual dark bronze-coloured Medicine Buddha in an antique shop a few months ago. He had a bowl of medicine on his lap and held an oversized pearl in his right hand, pinched gracefully between his thumb and forefinger. At the time of buying him, I was struggling with a relationship with a colleague who was very upset with me. I've always found it difficult when people are upset with me, and in this relationship it was coming up more strongly than ever before. When I examined what was happening, I could see that their dislike triggered a young part of me that felt utterly worthless. To protect me from this horrible feeling another part, a people-pleasing part, leapt in and worked really hard to get the other person to change their mind about me. If they didn't dislike me, I wouldn't have to feel worthless. The problem with this is that in those moments I can't access any of the other parts of me – the parts that know I am enough, the parts that remember that I am loved – and so I am either stuck in people-pleasing or I feel young, alone, and completely at the other person's mercy.

It felt like the Medicine Buddha had come into my life to help me with this relationship difficulty. I read up on him and found one of his mantras in Sanskrit, and I chanted it for hours. I also found myself intrigued by the position my Medicine Buddha was sitting in. He had such poise. I focussed on the pearl in his right hand. What did it represent? Or, more importantly, what did it represent to me?

I decided that, for me, the pearl represented all the other parts of me that I couldn't access when my worthless part was triggered. The worthless part of me felt very young, but I wasn't young now, and I also contain parts that can be compassionate, parts that can stand up for me, and parts that could understand why people say hurtful things. I could use the pearl to represent these parts, and hold them in front of me to

159

remind the worthless part that it wasn't alone. I ordered some big marbles from 'House of Marbles' online and chose one I liked – a clear one with an opalescent sheen. I took the pose of the mudra, and I invited the Medicine Buddha to join me. I felt present, strong, and gentle. I felt like I could hold myself steady in this position, with all my other parts held so visibly in front of me, and the Medicine Buddha behind me.

As I sat in front of the Medicine Buddha in my office that evening, my stomach cramping, it was clear that there was something I hadn't 'digested' from the day. I wondered if it might have been the interaction with the angry woman. I got out my marble, took the position of the Medicine Buddha, and invited him to sit with me – a reassuring and holding presence.

The tears started flowing almost immediately. The word she used had really hurt me. It had pierced me – an arrow of hate that had taken me unawares and travelled right into the young worthless part. I kept thinking, 'ouch!' I cried for myself, and then for the young part of me, who I hadn't looked after properly in my people-pleasing part's hurry to start convincing the angry woman to like me. I had lost my marble and I hadn't even realised until eight hours later.

I gave attention to the young part of me, and I felt myself loved by the Medicine Buddha. The young part started feeling better, and my indigestion eased. I even became curious about the woman – what threat did we represent to her? How might we have triggered parts of her that felt unsafe?

I will continue to go to the Medicine Buddha when I need help in these difficult interactions. I'm sure I'll forget my marble again, and become overwhelmed by the one or two parts of me that are triggered into working so hard that they overwhelm me. That's okay. I can remember the other parts of me later. I can offer loving attention to the parts that were scared, and feel them bathed in the Buddha's light. I'll chant the Medicine Buddha's healing mantra, and keep stepping forward into this scary and wonderful world.

On being changed

I've been reflecting on how I've changed over the past twenty years. In some ways, I'm the same old person. I still love to read and write, and I have a joyful connection with cats. I still hate exercise. My hair is still (apart from a little grey) the same colour. I have the same laugh.

In other ways, I'm completely transformed. I was an atheist and I'm now a Buddhist priest. During those twenty years I trained as a psychotherapist and I wrote seven books. I lived in two houses I owned, and rented many others. I left an eleven year relationship and then got married to someone else. I moved here to run the temple.

Today, I live my life from an almost completely different set of principles. I used to want fame and money and praise – and I often still want those things, but at least now I know that they won't bring me happiness. These days I am more relaxed, less codependent, more humble (except when I'm not!), wiser, less needy and more full of faith. Am I more happy? I think I am. And I'm still transforming all the time.

How did these dramatic changes come about?

Well, I'd like to take all the credit. I've worked hard. I've been in and out of therapy over the years – in fact I'm starting some work with a new therapist next week. I've spent years in 12 step programmes. I have read hundreds, probably thousands of books. I have done countless hours of Buddhist practice. I have learnt from many teachers, Buddhist and otherwise, including a precious transmission from Dharmavidya, the head of our Order.

But how can I take the credit, when this list is completely comprised of what I've received from others? How much of other people's love and wisdom I've absorbed over the years! I have received so much that I couldn't even begin to express it to you. From my parents to the purring cat at my feet right now, I've had helping hands every step of the way.

I did play my part in this process. I forced myself to go, trembling, to my first 12 step meeting. I turned up at the dreaded therapy session. I listened to the feedback I didn't want to hear, and studied, and paid money to go on courses, and learnt from different workplaces, and tried really hard to improve.

The more I reflect, though, I'm not sure how much of this I can take credit for either. My conditions made it possible for me to have the life I've had, and to make the choices I've made. Who started the 12 step movement? Not me. Who wrote the books, built the University, made the money to buy this temple, invented this computer, painted our shrine room, gave the teachings that I pass on in my Dharma talks? Not me.

"The light will work its own good work
if only we will trust it..."
from Tai Shi Chih's prayer in the Amida Shu Nien Fo book

In my experience, the more I trust the Buddha, and allow myself to be led by the golden light, the more effectively he is able to change me.

The Buddha knows what changes to make next, and at what speed those changes need to happen. He knows better than I do. There's no point in blasting an unripe plum with intense light and heat – it will ripen better in the sun, in its own time.

What we can do is turn our faces towards the light, like flowers. This is what I do whenever I say the nembutsu. What we can do is put in the legwork – by asked trusted people what we should do, and then doing it, whether we want to or not. Beyond that, our fate is in the laps of the Buddhas. Maybe we'll manifest a published book or children or a business or a beautiful garden. Maybe we won't. It's all okay, because we can trust the light. We can keep an open mind, and be patient. We can allow the Buddha to heal us.

Morning yoga

I've had a complicated history with exercise. My Physical Education teachers at school thought it was helpful to push their students past their limits, and this was extremely unhelpful for me. It left me with lots of associations between exercise and failure, and exercise and powerlessness. I experienced certain horrible situations during school sports lessons as mildly traumatic, and this trauma experience repeats when I am in similar situations. I feel anxious when I get out of breath, and panicky when I think I might not be strong enough to do something. I generally experience a deep antipathy towards exercise, and an almost complete lack of faith in my body.

Over the years I have made various attempts to exercise with mixed results. I have gradually become more conscious of a part of me that consistently pushes my body beyond its limits. This is an unconscious 'repeat' of my childhood experience. It means that when I do go to exercise or yoga classes I've often made myself feel sick or dizzy, which then leads to feelings of panic. As this repeats it becomes more and more difficult to get myself back to the class and eventually I retreat, spending months or years without any exercise.

Over the past year I have been experimenting with yoga at home, with a clearer knowledge of my tendency to push myself too hard. I started with fifteen minutes a morning, at a beginner's level. This felt possible. I'm now doing half an hour of yoga a few mornings a week, at a level which includes some strength-building and cardiovascular work as well as flexibility and relaxation.

I am beginning to see my morning yoga as a kind of ballet. I enjoy making the movements as smoothly as I can, and noticing how my body is changing over time. When I'm on my yoga mat I avoid thinking about my day and instead am mindful of my physicality – concentrating on the sensation of being out of breath, or the deliciousness of twists and stretches. I feel grateful to my body with all its complexity, for carrying me and for keeping me alive.

I am beginning to take refuge in my body, as something I can lean into and trust. As I learn what my limits are, I can pull back before I reach them, or play around their edges a little more gently without driving myself beyond my limits, and falling into panic or anxiety.

Sometimes healing can takes decades or more. It helps when we begin to be aware of our wounds, and of the different parts of us that may be repeating these familiar patterns. It helps if we approach all the parts of ourselves with kindness and patience, listening to their experience and asking how we can help.

As I take refuge in my physicality, I become more present in the world. I am more embodied, and more a part of the earth beneath my feet. This 'joined up' feeling helps me to take refuge in the Buddha, as I feel her presence alongside me. Taking refuge in the Buddha helps me to take deeper refuge in my body. The virtuous circle continues.

With refuge we get happy

Happiness is a cornflower-blue butterfly landing on our wrist.

We can't manufacture or manipulate happiness, by following exactly the same recipe we used last time, or by going down the exact same path. We can't even prolong it by artificial means for very long, however much ice-cream we have to hand. Happiness has a mind of its own, like a cat.

Happiness likes to visit people who are relaxed. It prefers people who pay attention to what's around them, and people who are grateful. It isn't swayed by money or flattery, and it doesn't respond to bullying.

When we take refuge, we are slowly improving the conditions of our soil, and this makes it more likely that happiness will grow and blossom. This happens even when we are overwhelmed by a big grief or toxic resentment – happy will find nooks and crannies where it can send up flowers, even if they are small and white.

If you keep taking refuge, happy will visit you, sooner or later. It might even move in.

To rejoice

O crows circling over my head and cawing!
I admit to being, at times,
Suddenly, and without the slightest warning
Exceedingly happy.
~ Charles Simic

When we ordain as priests in my Buddhist tradition, Amida Shu, we vow to subscribe to one hundred and fifty six precepts. These precepts are inspirational and aspirational rather than prescriptive. We strive to 'not be opinionated' and 'to be neither grasping nor possessive', with a general understanding that we will fall short of keeping these precepts absolutely, sometimes many times in a single minute.

One of my favourite precepts is in the section titled 'on joy in the practice' and it is simply: 'to rejoice'. Partly I think that this precept works as a warning against taking ourselves too seriously as priests. Religion is a serious business, but if it becomes earnest at the cost of our sense of humour or a lightness of being, then I think that we are missing the point. I am more likely to trust religious leaders who have the ability to laugh heartily, or who at least have a semi-permanent twinkle in their eyes.

How is it to work with this precept? How can I aspire to experiencing more joy? Mostly, I find that making efforts to be more joyful doesn't seem to make much of a difference. Happiness often lands upon us when we are least expecting it, or concentrating on something else.

When we first started looking after the temple bunnies, I read that rabbits don't respond well to being wooed in the way we might woo a cat, by holding out our hand to them, or looking them in the eyes. As prey animals they are always on the look-out for creatures that might want to eat them. Staring a rabbit in the eyes or approaching it directly is what a hunting animal might do, and it makes them very nervous. Instead, the book suggested that you sit quietly somewhere near the rabbit, reading your book or somehow otherwise averting your eyes, and wait for the rabbit to come to you.

We can approach joy in the same way. We can let it know that it is welcome, but that we're not going to chase it or cling to it. We can do this by setting up various conditions in our lives. We can practise good self-care, and do good things for others. We can make Sabbath spaces in our schedules. We can pay proper attention to the world. We can be meticulously honest with ourselves, and feel contrition and say sorry when appropriate. We can put ourselves in the conditions that we know are good for us – walking in nature, Buddhist services, nice dinners out with our friends. We can practice gratitude (this one is very important). We can try and live good lives. We can take refuge in the five jewels – Amida, the Buddha, the Dharma, the Sangha and the Pure Land.

On a course I attended once, the poet Selima Hill commented that poems were simply a by-product of living-like-a-poet – like sloughed off snake-skins. If you go through your days paying a particular quality of attention, delighting in colours or being curious about people's inner lives, it is natural that you would write about these things and make the language as beautiful as you can. In a similar way, when we live a life centred around the kinds of things I list above (and you will have your own activities to add to the list), joy tends to be a natural consequence, a by-product.

It isn't possible to be happy all the time. When we are grieving it is harder to connect to joy, although it may be possible to experience brief moments of it even in the middle of deep distress. If it has been necessary for us to shut ourselves off from life to keep our sadness or anger at bay, we will also be closing our hearts to the possibility of joy. Compulsions and addictions can consume us and make us focus in on ourselves – we won't find any joy here, just temporary satiation leading to more craving. Other mental imbalances such as depression will have the same effect. If we're in those dark places, we can trust that the sunshine is there but that the clouds are particularly thick. It may be that healing is necessary before we can open our hearts up to joy. We can seek help, be patient, and trust that happiness will come again when the time is ripe.

When I followed the book's instructions and ignored our bunnies, they did eventually come over to me, and nudged my legs with their noses. These nudges are their way of making friends with me – checking me out, coming into relationship. It always feels like a great gift to receive them. There are things I can do to make it more likely – not run at them, be quiet, maybe sometimes hold a little rabbit treat in my hands – but the rabbits are very much in control. Every time they seek me out, it's a gift.

When joy visits us, it is proper that we feel gratitude. My position is that, as human beings, we are not entitled to anything. The world didn't ask for us to be born. Everything we receive is unearned – a grace. If we deeply examine our dependent condition we will begin to appreciate how much we do receive, and how little we've done in return. When we are visited by moments of joy or other feelings like contentment or tenderness, we can say 'thank you very much'. We can also honour these feelings by enjoying every last drop.

On being happysad

Yesterday I texted a friend and used the word happysad to describe how I was feeling, having heard good news from a friend who was dying.

This morning I sat in our dark shrine room for morning meditation and looked out of the big window behind our Buddha. There was mist pooled in the valley and yellow street lights were dotting the landscape. The sky started a dusky blue, and as time went on it began to lighten. The bottom edge of the clouds took on a pink glow which spread upwards and intensified until the clouds were luminous. By the time I left the room the sky was baby blue and the clouds had lost their blush. It was daytime.

I noticed the feeling that bloomed in me as I watched. It is what I feel when I am in contact with something beautiful. Look at the delicate line that aeroplane is tracing! Watch how the soft mist is thickening! Along with this sweetness, as if blue threads were woven into the same golden cloth, was regret and sadness. If the sadness could speak it would say something like, "I waste so much time in the tangles of my head, preoccupied with things that don't matter as much as noticing this sunrise." Also, "Everything comes to an end."

This bittersweet feeling has been written about by many Buddhist teachers, such as the Japanese poet Saigyo. Buddhism can bring us closer to an experience of the bittersweet because it doesn't let us forget impermanence. We are encouraged to open our eyes to the reality of life, which as Shakyamuni discovered includes the pain of birth, sickness, old age and death. We are encouraged to look behind our self-comforting delusions which keep us protected from the truth. We are asked to turn off the television, put our intoxicants down and face up to the discomfort of dukkha.

Ironically, if we really face dukkha then we are more likely to see sukha, sweetness, in the world around us. We can have a more authentic encounter with the Other, and the Other will always include a little sweetness stirred in with the sadness.

When someone is leaving us, we can remember the parts of them that we'll miss. When we step out of denial, we release energy and receive an expanded view of what's possible. We can let new knowledge in where we didn't before. When things die, they make space for new life.

You may become a connoisseur of happysad. It does have a certain piquancy, a completeness – maybe like a tasty meal of brown rice and vegetables instead of an oversweet cake that gives us a sugar hit but doesn't really nourish us. Happysad is the whole picture. It is the truth.

Everything I love will leave me or die, unless I leave first. What a terrible world. And how beautiful it is!

On luxury

Just now I snapped off a square of dark coffee chocolate and savoured the sweet creaminess as it melted on my tongue. Luxury. I am getting over a virus. Last night I was able to breathe clearly for the first time in days, and swallow without pain. My sleep was long and deep. Luxury. I have an hour before my next appointment, a good book, fairy lights are twinkling in the fireplace, and Tsuki cat is perched on the back of my chair purring. Perfect luxury.

What is luxury? Sylvain Tesson, who retreated to a tiny log cabin in the wild forests of Russia for six months, reflects on it here:

"The temperature drops precipitously. I chop down some wood in –31 F and when I get home, the heat seems like a supreme luxury. After the frigid air, the sound of a vodka cork popping near a cast-iron stove produces infinitely more pleasure than a palatial stay on the Grand Canal in Venice. That huts might rank with palaces is something the habitués of royal suites will never understand. They did not experience the aching of numbed fingers before they learned about bubble baths. Luxury is not a state but the crossing of a line, a threshold beyond which, suddenly, all suffering ceases."

What I find accurate about Tesson's definition of luxury is that he places it right next door to suffering. Luxury is when we move from the sun-baked lawn into the cool shade of a tree, or, when we begin to feel chilly, we move back into the sun. The cool is most delicious when we're a little over-heated.

Tesson also says that luxury is not a state – we can't linger there forever. As we move away from suffering, the luxury either becomes boring, or we move into an opposite state of suffering. Sunsets and cherry blossom are beautiful because of their transience – even cherry blossom would become commonplace if we were wading through it all year long. Tsuki is still purring, but I stopped paying attention to her a long time ago. Having a nap is a luxury when we are exhausted, but if we lie around all day, we can fall into a lazy torpor which is just as unpleasant as feeling tired.

The Buddha taught that we expend a lot of fruitless energy grabbing at the things we like, and pushing away those we don't like. When it comes to luxury we are often greedy for more, chasing luxury 'highs' and wanting to be in control of how much we receive. My top drawer is full of all sorts of different chocolate – coffee, mint, coconut... but at the moment the exact chocolate I want is the one I don't have – dark with sea salt. Once we start grabbing at luxury there is no end to it – just look at the lifestyles of some (not always happy) millionaires.

We can also use luxury-seeking as a way of pushing away the things we don't want to experience – sadness, confusion, or a sense of failure. We 'treat ourselves' to a bottle of wine rather than tending to our tiredness after a punishing week, or acknowledging the pain we're still feeling after an argument with our friend.

Luxury (along with pretty much everything else) wasn't designed to be something we can control. Luxury is a grace. If suffering is inevitable, and so is impermanence, then we are in constant motion between suffering and the cessation of suffering. Cold, warm, cold. Hungry, full, hungry again... Sad, happy, sad, happy. If we can be present for the suffering, we can also be present for the luxury of 'the crossing of a line'.

In my own experience, the best kinds of luxury are the very ordinary things that we receive every day, mostly without noticing. If we are present for our lives, we will feel a deep gratitude at the cup of tea our husband offers us, and relish the hot liquid as it soothes our sore throat. We will luxuriate in feeling loved by a friend when they text us, in pausing to watch the sun disappear behind the hill, and in putting on our soft warm pyjamas after a long day of work (one of my favourites). When we remove the scales from our eyes, we see that we are blessed.

I wish for you the courage to stay present with your suffering. Let your breath out. I wish for you the joys of a thousand tiny luxuries. Let the air, rich with oxygen, stream into your lungs by itself.

With refuge we become kinder

When we fail to be kind, it is because we are afraid.

We are afraid of using up our resources, and being left without. We are afraid of being taken advantage of, or that the other person will become reliant on our ongoing help. We are afraid of looking silly or getting it wrong or of not receiving the appreciation we 'deserve'.

Sometimes we fail to be kind because we need to defend an image of ourselves, or prop ourselves up by putting someone else down.

When we take refuge, it becomes easier to notice what needs doing, and to simply do it. We open the door for the woman struggling with a pushchair not because we want to look like a nice person, but because we can see that she needs it to be done. We give away the last jar of our homemade jam because it will make our friend happy and we know that there will be more next year.

We don't become angels. We are careful to notice our limits, because pushing too far beyond them isn't helpful for us or for the person we are helping. We acknowledge that we can't do everything that needs doing. We weep for all the suffering in the world, and we acknowledge that we will continue to add to this, both consciously and unconsciously. We do what we can.

Whenever we fail to be kind, it is because we lack courage – and refuge gives us courage. When we take refuge, we become kinder. We then discover that being kind makes us happy.

On being kind to wasps

Over the past few weeks, the shrine room has been filling with dying wasps. They come through the cracks and cluster around the shrine by the big windows, slowly crawling on the curtains or curling into sleep on the carpet. It sometimes makes morning meditation quite hazardous, as I keep one eye shut and one eye on the wasp that has started to crawl under my left knee...

I'm not a big fan of wasps. These particular wasps have already stung two of our templemates. One stung Brian on the hand whilst doing a very good impression of being dead, or maybe it had already died and its venom sac was still pulsing. One stung Carine on the sole of her foot when she was trying to take them out to a quiet place in the garden to die.

In terms of my feelings towards them, I'd put them in the same category as the plump slugs that find their way into our flat and trail slime all over the cat biscuits at night, and the huge rats that are currently living in our compost heap. They are inconvenient at best. At worst they are repulsive, and inspire feelings of hate in me.

During this morning's meditation I noticed a petal on the carpet, fallen from the flowers on the shrine. As I watched, a few of the wasps clustered around it. I realised that they were hungry. I had the thought, "I don't want them to die hungry". This thought was accompanied by a flush of compassion – fellow feeling for wasps. I know how it is to be hungry. I know how it is to be helpless, and desperate.

Of course, I may be taking my anthropomorphising too far. I read later that worker wasps only live an average of a few weeks, and that they all die because of a lack of food rather than the cold. I have been watching natural deaths for wasps. Do wasps and other insects feel pain? This is a question that has been long debated by scientists and biological ethicists – they certainly don't feel it in the same way that we do.

Were the wasps I watched really seeking traces of nectar on the fallen petal? Were they exhibiting a mechanical drive to survive? Did they enjoy some last sweetness? Who knows? I watched, and I made some assumptions and guesses – something we do whenever we encounter another being's behaviour. I imagined how it might be to die of hunger, and I felt compassion. I even briefly entertained the idea of bringing them some food, knowing that beginning the task of feeding hungry insects would lead me to madness. I felt kindly towards these wasps, and I wished that their deaths be easy.

It is easy to feel compassion when a dear friend is suffering through a divorce, or when we see footage of children caught up in war. It can be more of a challenge to feel compassion towards an addicted son who lies and cheats, a spoilt rich banker who falls on hard times, ourselves when we let ourselves down, or wasps. This is where compassion becomes an advanced practice, and compassion can't be forced. It either arises or it doesn't.

If I hadn't been settled quietly on my meditation cushion, I may not have been attentive to the behaviour of the wasps. To imagine how it is to be someone else, we need to feel secure enough to take our eyes off ourselves and look outside. We need some energy and some capacity. We need to have taken refuge in something sturdier than our own whims. The deeper the refuge, the more friendly we can feel towards wasps, and everything else.

How to help according to Dogen

Last week I was standing in a long queue at the airport, waiting to board my plane. I was travelling with a budget airline and so only the people in the front half of the queue would get to keep their free hand luggage on the plane. We stood there patiently or impatiently for forty minutes.

I was reading a book about yoga on my kindle. At one point I looked down and found that my left arm had somehow snaked underneath my right and was holding onto my coat. This meant that my right wrist, the one holding the weight of the kindle, was perfectly supported by my left. It was a very comfortable and sustainable position for reading in a queue, and I wondered how on earth my left arm had made the decision to do it.

Years ago I read a koan presented in Dogen's Shobogenzo which has stayed with me. The koan, which is called 'The Hands and Eyes of Great Compassion', starts like this:

Yunyan asks Daowu: "How does the Bodhisattva of Great Compassion use so many hands and eyes?"
Daowu said: "It's just like a person in the middle of the night reaching back in search of a pillow."

The Bodhisattva of Great Compassion is also known as Quan Yin, Avalokiteshvara, or the 'Hearer of the Cries of the World'. She (or he) has many hands and eyes so she can provide assistance wherever help is needed. We have a deep connection with Quan

Yin in my Buddhist tradition. When I look up from my desk, I can see a picture of her hanging above my shrine in all her golden beauty. She has a soft, comforting energy and we often suggest that people who are suffering use her chant to call on her energy.

When I hear Daowu explain how Quan Yin manages to handle all her different hands and eyes, without getting things wrong and without tiring, I think of my left arm, coming in to support my kindle without me asking it. Some part of my body or mind noticed that I needed something – a way of reading comfortably in the queue – and so a solution was found without me needing to get involved. This is how we reach back for a pillow in the night – our hand is hardly conscious of what it's doing, but it's doing what needs to be done.

We can help other people in this way. We can pass the salt to someone sitting across from us because we can see they are looking for it. We can reach out to catch a child who is falling, or offer a hug to someone who has been through a trauma. When we help in this way we don't expect anything back in return, and we don't tire. We simply do what needs to be done without any fuss.

Of course, we are bombu – foolish beings of wayward passion – and we rarely meet the ideal shown to us by Quan Yin. Sometimes I help because I like to see myself as helpful, or because I want the other person to like me. Sometimes I want them to feel like they owe me. Most of our helping is tainted with self-serving aspirations like these – some of them conscious, some not.

That's okay. It's (usually) still better to help than not to help, regardless of our motivations. It's always good to get clearer about our different motivations, as this helps them to dissolve away. We can also trust that, if we put our anxious and grabbing egos to one side, helping will become more natural. Jesus told us that his yoke was light. If we allow the energy of Quan Yin to flow through us, we'll have plenty of energy for doing what needs to be done. This kind of helping leaves no trace. I'm grateful to my left arm for helping me out, but it doesn't need any thanks. It was happy to be there, propping my right arm up. Can we let our whole beings be like this, with eyes and arms everywhere?

Selling bitter medicine

Every Saturday evening we hold something called a Nembutsu Circle here at the temple. In this practice we sit in a circle and take turns holding a big smooth stone. Whoever is holding the stone can speak or sit in silence, and everyone else is quiet. This simple exercise always results in a deeply sacred space, no matter who is present, and I find it one of the most helpful practices we do.

The Nembutsu Circle is our least popular offering. There are different reasons for this, but the biggest is that it asks people to become vulnerable. It is a rare thing to be truly listened to. Sometimes people are shocked by the strength of anger or loneliness that wells up when they hold the stone, or they find tears running down their cheeks. There is nowhere to hide, and the attention and care of others in the circle can be almost too much.

My husband Kaspa and I have spent a good deal of time thinking about how we can attract people to the various events we offer here. We've tried all sorts of different things to advertise the Nembutsu Circle. Over the years I have experienced some frustration about the continuing low attendance. Yes, people might find the 'medicine' bitter to begin with, but it will offer them so much! The gift of being listened to is so precious, and when they listen to others they will hear just what they need to bring them courage, new insight and hope. I know for a fact that people would find it deeply helpful to come, if only I could find the right words to persuade them.

Or do I? In the 12 steps programmes they encourage 'attraction, not promotion'. This is a description of the correct way to spread the word about the benefits of the programmes. It is suggested that we don't set about using all our manipulative powers to get our friends to come. Instead we quietly and modestly continue to work our own programme. As we are slowly transformed by the work we do, those around us start getting curious. They might notice that we've started to set healthy boundaries, or that we seem happier. When they ask us what we're doing, we can let them know about the group we've been attending, and if they ask more questions, they can come along and find out for themselves.

In my experience, this gentle approach also works well for me as a vegan who has a deep wish for others to eat more vegan food. In my early days of veganism, still full of guilt for my years of contributing to animal suffering, I mentioned my new diet at every opportunity. I shared lots of shocking, gory videos on Facebook and I told my friends 'cruelty facts' while we were eating. I don't think I did much to advance the cause. I could easily have been put into the category of 'another one of those judgemental, angry food fascists'. I wouldn't have wanted to emulate me! If I want a role-model I think of my friend Lizzy, who quietly went about eating her delicious-looking vegan food for years before I became vegan. I was always inspired by her, and interested in what she ate, but she never forced her ideology on me.

I think that we need to be ripe before we say 'yes' to the discomfort that will lead to true change. This is true of someone making big changes to their diet, entering therapy, acknowledging that they have an addiction, joining a new spiritual group or attending a Nembutsu Circle. Pushing and shoving people doesn't help them to ripen more quickly. It might help them to spend time with people who are engaged in this kind of change, like putting an under-ripe peach into a paper bag of ripe bananas, but we can't exude ripeness on purpose or at will. We just have to go about our own spiritual practice or recovery, and remember that there are plenty of things for us to work on before we begin poking our nose into other people's lives and deciding what's best for them. (This last sentence is also a note to self!)

And so I will continue to search for the right words to describe the benefits of the Nembutsu Circle, but I won't worry too much about how many people turn up. The important thing is that I keep attending myself, and that I keep doing my own work. I've developed a taste for this bitter medicine, and it's delicious. If you want to try a swig sometime, just let me know.

With refuge we stop blaming

Blaming can feel delicious and awful, like scratching itchy skin too hard. It's even sweeter when others join us in our blaming.

We blame to protect ourselves. We don't want to discover the truth about ourselves or someone else. We don't want to feel vulnerable. We don't want to admit that we can't trust ourselves, so we see the problem as outside of us instead. We need an outlet for our rage or desperate disappointment.

Blame is connected to responsibility – who is responsible for this mistake? When we blame, we are saying that the other has, at best, made a stupid mistake they could have avoided, and at worst, intentionally hurt us or others. We say, 'if only you were different, I would be okay'.

That may be true. We may have an easier life if our partner did the washing up more often, or if our boss gave us more praise. The trouble with blame is that we are attempting to control something we are not in control of – other people. Once we've made a request, given our feedback, and been clear about our boundaries, then the rest of it is out of our hands.

When we point the finger at someone else, there are three fingers pointing back at us. What would we do differently next time? Do we regret any of our behaviour, even if the other person 'asked for it' or behaved extremely badly themselves? What boundaries didn't we set for ourselves? Can we see that the other person has poked a very sore wound in us, possibly without even realising? How can we take responsibility for our wound and take care of ourselves?

Sometimes people are worried that taking radical responsibility means letting the other person off the hook or allowing them to 'get away with it'. Maybe it does – that's okay, we don't need to concern ourselves with their choices. In my experience, however, nobody is exempt from experiencing the consequences of their actions. Denial only works for so long. Generally, people who manage their lives by 'getting away with it' are not happy people. How they deal with their karma is not our business.

It takes courage to step out of blame. First we have to let go of the illusion of control, which has kept us feeling safe. Then we usually have to take responsibility for some of what happened. Even when we had no part in what happened, for example if someone stole our handbag from us in the street, we can begin to see the assault more as an unlucky 'act of nature' rather than something personal, and take responsibility for tending our bruises.

The safer we feel to start with, the easier it will be to let go of another prized piece of our self-image and admit to our part. The more deeply we take refuge, the safer we feel.

Who's done this to me?

This morning, after letting the temple bunnies out of their hutch, I wandered down into the garden.

There were holes gouged into the entire length of our lawn. Deep holes. The turf from each hole had been tossed aside and was dying in the cold air. These holes had been slowly appearing for months, but last night was a disaster – this morning there were almost more dark holes than there was green grass.

If I thought that someone was sneaking into our garden late at night with the intent of ruining our garden, I would be furious. How dare they! Who's done this to me? How can I get my revenge?

Instead, I know that the culprit is a black and white scoundrel with fur who is looking for his dinner. Badgers need worms to eat, and our lawn must be a particularly rich feasting ground. I survey the holes, halfheartedly attempting to fill them in with my boot, and gently curse him. "Oh, Badger... you've really made a mess this time." I hope he went away with a full belly.

I am reminded of the traditional Zen/Taoist story of the man who is furious when a boat appears out of nowhere and collides with his own newly painted boat, despite his warning yells. He is full of anger, that is, until he sees that there is nobody in the boat. It is empty.

Our lawn holes weren't made by a malicious being wanting to make work for us – they are the side effect of his or her hunger. No one in the boat. Even if there was someone in the boat, maybe they were tired and made a mistake. Maybe they have poor eye-sight. Maybe they had a terrible day, and in that moment they didn't care about our boat, so desperate were they to get home. It's still an empty boat.

What if the other person does set out to cause us harm? What if it is personal? Maybe they're jealous of our lovely boat and they want to mess it up. Maybe they think we slighted them at work or treated their sister badly, and they follow us out onto the water. Maybe they just have it in for people with red hair.

Whatever their reasons, we can be sure that it is none of our business. If they feel we have done them an injustice, we should scrupulously examine our own side of the street, and make amends if we have acted unskilfully in any way. We could let them know how it was for us, and state our needs. We need to make sure we're safe, by setting appropriate boundaries. We may feel able to offer the other person help, by giving their hurt or angry parts empathy, or by offering practical help. Once we've done these things, we are powerless over the rest. We can hand the karma of the boat-bashing person back to them, and (if we're really on our way towards being enlightened!) wish them well. We can let them go. We can release ourselves. It's not personal, even when it is.

We all get trapped in the heat of 'who's done this to me?' many times a day. My husband has left his clothes on the floor again! She should have known how much that comment would hurt me! They always expect me to change my plans! What an idiot driver, they could have killed me!

When you find yourself getting ready to scream at the person in the boat, see if you can pause and consider that it may be empty. The other person is doing what they're doing for a complex set of reasons, some of which will be unknown to us and to them. Who knows how much knowledge they have of the impact they're having? Who knows how difficult it would be for them to make a different choice? Leave them to experience the consequence of their behaviour, and enjoy the holes in the lawn. Maybe we could make it into a crazy golf course...

The gap between the ideal and the actual

I'm away on a writing retreat and, shortly after finishing my introduction to this section on blaming, I received an email from a family member which felt like a punch in the stomach. It knocked me sideways. I spent some time trying to process my feelings. I called a friend and talked it through. I wrote to a couple of other friends. I made efforts to understand where the other person was coming from, and to try and make sense of the fuzzy shroud of confusion around me. I made a decision to hand my feelings back to the other person. None of it worked.

It is helpful to be reminded, whilst writing this book, of the huge gap between the ideal and the actual, between the theory and the practice. It is all very well to read lots of books, study psychotherapy and psychology, train as a Buddhist priest and come up with neat ideas about how human beings work and what is helpful for them. It is entirely another thing when I am lying in bed late at night with my eyes wide open, my previously-neat bedroom strewn with clothes and debris, considering getting the chocolate biscuits out of my luggage (I did).

Our suffering goes deep, like magma. As I write this, I am still erupting and I know the truth of it. Tomorrow or maybe the day after, I will forget the intensity and be left with a shadow of this knowing. It is painful to be human, and most of us move in and out of denial. This is why we trust that Amitabha sees the depth of our suffering, just as it is, and can offer us consolation. Sometimes we are lucky enough to find people who really get what we're going through, but when we don't, we can show our wounds to Amida and see that she understands.

When I received that difficult email, one thing did eventually help me more than anything else. That thing was taking refuge. I took myself off to a bench at the top of a slope that overlooks the valley, and I shut my eyes. I went into an imaginary room with the Medicine Buddha, who has helped me in similar situations in the past, and I visualised the person who wrote the email coming into the room with us. This put me in touch with a part of me that was deeply frightened. It was tiny, like an underdeveloped shrimp. I heard it, reassured it, and it began to grow. Once it felt better, I began to feel calmer, and I was able to be curious about the other person's process.

It would be very easy to create a story about this person 'ruining my writing retreat'. They did something to me, didn't they? When I felt calmer, I could see that this person's flailing about has caught a vulnerable part of me 'by mistake'. Their behaviour was an attempt at keeping themselves together. Even if they intended me harm (which I don't think they did), I am only a stand-in for someone else – probably someone from their distant past. It's never really personal.

My responsibility when I'm triggered into extreme feelings is to do what I need to do to reconnect with the other parts of me, and a sense of groundedness. This might mean taking some time out, asking friends to support me, talking it through in therapy or anything that helps me to look after my vulnerable shrimp part. Only when I have found some equilibrium will I begin to wonder what I want to do about the situation – whether I want to give feedback, or set a boundary, or step back from the relationship altogether. Once I've found the ground under my feet again, I will focus on my own needs and limitations rather than on their faults. I will be more able to be kind if I do set boundaries, and maybe I'll even be able to support them in their process, which I suspect will be equally painful in some way.

I don't want to tie this story up too neatly – partly because it isn't neatly tied up, and partly because I want to stay open to the reality of the messiness of being human. Sometimes the gap between the ideal and the actual is at least the size of the Grand Canyon.

Whether we can feel it at the time or not, I trust that Amida is bigger.

On gratitude towards our tormentors

Last year I found myself in terrible tangles in a relationship with a colleague. We rubbed each other up the wrong way, and I began to feel very unsafe around him.

As time went on I found myself thinking about the relationship more and more, and talking to people about what was happening at every opportunity. I noticed that when I had these conversations, one of my favourite bits was telling the other person how awful this person was being. I would give examples of things they'd done, highlighting certain actions for maximum effect, and when they made sympathetic noises or agreed that they were terrible, I felt a sick pleasure and a great relief.

The relief was the kind you feel when you go shopping to try and salve a broken heart. It was never enough. It lasted for a while, but then I had to find someone new to talk to, or wait for this person to do something else that infuriated me or demonstrated the depths of his unreasonableness.

I was engaged in blaming as an attempt at keeping myself safe. I needed him to be wrong so I wasn't wrong. I needed him to be the bad guy so I wasn't the bad girl. And, deep down, a part of me was certain that I was terrible. This part of me knew I was despicable – evil, manipulative, unworthy, the dirt under your feet. I was desperate to get away from that feeling. Somehow I had given him the power to decide whether it was true or not. When he treated me well, I was okay. When he treated me badly, it was irrevocable evidence to that unworthy part that all the 'good' people saw in me was a trick. At my core I was rotten.

The relationship dynamics we get tangled up in can be hugely powerful. They can pull on parts of us that go right down into our roots, where our survival mechanisms were fashioned under great pressure. This pressure is the difference between being accepted and nourished as a helpless infant, or abandoned to an early death. It is unlikely that our parents would actually have left us on a hillside to die, but when we are young and they get angry at us and leave us for a while, we don't know that they're coming back. When a minor issue in a relationship feels like a life or death issue, it probably was – and still is to that young part of you.

It's no good pretending that young part isn't there. I tried this, along with all the other things I could think of. I learnt how to communicate with him using non-violent communication, and that helped. I learnt more about the part of me that felt worthless by listening to it and empathising with it, and that helped. I set some practical boundaries for myself around this person, and that helped.

It's not fixed. I still get extremely triggered around this person. I still find myself falling into blaming: "If they did this differently, then everything would be okay." I still find myself seeking allies as a way of propping up my righteousness: "They did this. Aren't they awful?" I find myself people-pleasing around him, as an attempt at manipulating his experience of me so I can feel better about myself.

I notice when I fall into blaming, and sometimes I am able to step back. I remember that this person doesn't actually have any power over me, only the power I've given him. I remember that I can look after myself better these days, and that I'm no longer two years old. I remember that he has his own reasons for the way he behaves around me, and that maybe I'm just as strong a trigger for him as he is for me.

It is easier for me to let go of blaming when I feel that something else is propping me up instead. This something is refuge. Amida illuminates the parts of me that blame or people-please, and she understands and accepts these parts. She illuminates the part of me that thinks it's worthless, and she understands and accepts it. She knows that I will probably continue to be triggered, and that's okay. As I feel more okay about being utterly worthless, I become less afraid of touching into that part of me. The less afraid I am, the less effect this person has on me. I see myself more accurately, as a mixture of good and bad, light and dark. Just like everyone else.

On a psychotherapy course I went on, they talked about the people we find really difficult, our tormentors, as our best mentors. These tormentors show us something that no one else can. In this case, my colleague shows me the part of me that is convinced of my awfulness. It really is disgusted at itself. I feel sad for it as I write. It is very alone. Other parts of me have been working hard for decades to cover it up, so other people don't see it and reject me, and so I don't feel overwhelmed by the emotion it holds.

Most of the time, I don't like that this colleague shows me this worthless part. My system is still working hard to keep me away from it. As time goes on, and as I continue to take refuge, my defences will continue to be softened by love. This worthless part will begin to heal. One day, I will move away from blame and towards gratitude.

With refuge we can handle difficulty

Once we've taken refuge, the difficult stuff doesn't stop happening.

Refuge reminds us that everything passes.

Refuge helps us to see that we only suffer when we cling.

Refuge gives us a place to catch our breath before we go back into the whirl of the storm.

Refuge reminds us that we will survive this and, even when we don't, that will be okay too.

Refuge brings us solace.

Refuge is bigger than anything else that could ever happen to us, even if we can't believe it at the time.

We can rest in refuge.

On resisting change

For a couple of months, Kaspa had been mentioning changing the layout of our shrine room.

I didn't want to change the shrine room around. The shrine room had been arranged in a certain way since we moved into the temple four years ago, and it worked very well. I was used to it, and so was everyone else who comes to services here. I didn't think that his suggestion would work, and so whenever he mentioned it I made vaguely encouraging noises and hoped he'd forget about it.

Yesterday morning he came into my office and said he'd rearranged all the chairs and cushions, and did I want to have a look. I went upstairs to the shrine room with him and, as I stepped into the room, I felt my hackles rising.

I put forward my objections as I saw them. There would be no room to do walking meditation if the meditation cushions were there. This person was in the way of the ancestor shrine. Those people at the back wouldn't be able to hear the Dharma talk if we sat all the way over here. There wouldn't be enough chairs if the Sangha carried on growing.

Kaspa patiently dealt with my objections one by one. We made some more rearrangements, and began to work out how we might move around the room. I slowly felt my obstinacy softening, and allowed that we could keep it as it was for that evening's service, just to see how it worked.

By the time our usual Wednesday night congregants arrived, I was already coming round to the benefits of the new layout. Rather than sitting in rows like for a class or a show, everyone sat around the edges of the walls, facing each other in a kind of circle. Rather than the chairs obscuring the beautiful Amida Buddha at the back of the shrine room, we were now including both him and the standing Shakyamuni Buddha, with a clear stretch of room joining them to each other and to the view across the valley. Rather than being able to 'hide at the back', congregants were right in the middle of the room – participants rather than observers.

Yes, my seat was in a strange place in the room, just where the door opened and people came in. How did it feel? I felt vulnerable, and that was okay. I joked that this was my job as a priest – to sit in the awkward place, and to hold the space steady.

One of our congregants hated the new layout so much that she came out of the shrine room to tell me before the start of service. She felt exposed and anxious. I gave her a hug and reassured her. My Dharma talk that night was, of course, about how we resist change – how it makes us vulnerable, and threatens our efforts at self-building and seeking security. I talked about how this vulnerability gives us a new opportunity to let the Buddha in, and, most of all, that we weren't alone in the shrine room or anywhere – that the Buddhas were with us.

By the time the kettle had boiled after service everyone, including the congregant who had a strong negative reaction, the one who usually hates change, and me, felt pleased with the new layout. We acknowledged that it would take some getting used to, and that there were some issues to iron out. We also all found things that we liked about it.

We become attached to things so easily, including our religious rituals and practices. Sometimes it is good to do things the same way – to increase the power of ritual by repetition and familiarity, and to remind us how safe we are when we hang out with the Buddha. Sometimes we need everything to change so that what-doesn't-change comes into sharper focus. As we sit in our new seats, feeling wobbly, refuge will help us.

My magic mala

Let me show you my mala.

A mala is a special string of beads which Buddhists have traditionally used to keep track of mantras, breaths, prostrations, or anything else that needs to be counted. They often have one hundred and eight beads, a traditional sacred number, and mine is a 'half mala' so has fifty four. They are often made of wood or precious stones – mine's made of beautiful red carnelian beads, with colours ranging from pale translucent amber to deep glossy brick.

Every morning, I use this mala to count my nembutsu. After lighting an incense stick and bowing to my golden Buddha, I sit in the bucket chair in my office and look out of the window. We are moving towards autumn, but it is still light when I get up at 6.45am, and I can look out across the valley and watch the birds as they come to the feeder. Sometimes there is a squirrel.

Namo Amida Bu, Namo Amida Bu, Namo Amida Bu, Namo Amida. Fifty four times, using the tune we use when we do prostrations in the shrine room. It takes about five minutes. I have a tendency to put a lot of pressure on myself when it comes to starting good habits. If the new habit feels like too much of a stretch, a rebellious part pops up to counter the pressure, and I drop the habit. Aiming for five minutes feels very possible, and so the part that puts on pressure and the part that rebels aren't activated. Doing five minutes of nembutsu every day almost always feels possible.

When I travel, I take my mala with me. Last year I took it to a big meeting full of powerful people where there was a lot of conflict. I put it in my trouser pocket and, when I felt a little overwhelmed, I reached in and felt the beads between my fingertips. I also reached for it when the atmosphere in the room got very ugly, and it gave me the courage to stand up and shakily raise my voice.

I took it when I accompanied a friend to hospital so she could get an unpleasant test. Hospitals scare me, and it was important that I could be steady for her, and my mala helped. I take it away on writing retreat with me, and it reminds me of the Buddha when I face the terror of the blank page. I have it in my pocket at the start of the Buddhist retreats I lead, when the room is full of people and I want to get everything right.

As time goes on, I have discovered that this mala has special powers. When I run my fingers over the cool beads, I feel grace touching me. Of course, it is only an object. One day I will lose it or, if I manage to keep hold of it, after outliving me it will eventually wear away into dust. In the meantime, though, it connects me to the strength of our Sangha and our teacher. It connects me to the practice I've done in the past, and to all the Dharma I've absorbed over the years. It connects me to Amitabha.

As I make the physical connection between my body and the weight of the beads, a spiritual connection also opens up. I feel courage streaming through me. These things are with me in the room, contained in my sacred object. It is my transitional object, just like a child's blanket or beloved soft toy.

As I continue to take refuge, more and more of the objects around me take on a similar power. My candle has the power to help me write, and my beautiful mug helps me to relax even when I simply look at it. Looking at the bench outside brings me spaciousness. Smelling incense takes me into the Buddha's lap. As we feel more at home in the world, we become braver. We know that we are safe, and so there is nothing to lose. It's not just my mala that's magic. It's everything.

On getting stung

As the summer progresses, a steady stream of wasps are continuing to make their way into the shrine room from their nest on the balcony. Some of them are livelier than others, and this morning we did our walking meditation very carefully around the back of the Buddha where they are all congregating. I exchanged worried looks with our bell-master as we hoped that they would all stay where they were and not sting someone who was visiting us for the first time. It wouldn't have been a good start.

At the end, after prostrations, we sat around the shrine and Kaspa gave a Dharma talk. As he told a story about Ippen, I watched a wasp as it crawled from behind the shrine onto the shrine carpet and towards Kaspa and the rest of the congregation.

When I first became a Buddhist, I liked the idea that the Buddha could keep us safe from things like wasp stings. If we took refuge in him, surely he could use some of his superpowers to keep us from harm, or at least to make things less uncomfortable? We are sitting in front of him after an hour of practice – surely he could stretch to keeping this single wasp from getting too close?

Nick Cave sang, "I don't believe in an interventionist God", and I'm mostly with him. The Buddha cannot prevent all suffering and injustice. There are stories of the mystical Buddha intervening in people's lives, but generally it seems that he's not here to prevent our discomfort, but to help us to bear it with more courage and dignity. This is what the teaching of the noble truths tells us – we cannot avoid suffering, but with the help of the Buddhas we can transform our energetic response to it into good action.

If the Buddha can't stop us from being stung, then how will taking refuge help us? Well, taking refuge will help me to have compassion towards the wasps, as you've already read in the 'kindness' section. This alters my experience of being alongside the wasps this morning – they have as much right to be in our shrine room as we do, really, and as long as they're not bothering us I feel okay about sharing it. Taking refuge might also help me to feel more grounded and to be more mindful, which might make it less likely that I get stung – flailing around enrages wasps and makes a sting more likely.

The biggest benefit, it seems to me, is that refuge reminds us that whatever happens, we will be okay. Maybe the wasp will sting me, and maybe it won't. Either way, I will be held by the Buddha's compassion. I will be able to remember that the pain will pass, and that I will heal. Even if the very worst was to happen and my wasp bite got infected and I died, I would still be okay – the Buddha will look after me when I've died. Whatever this looks like in reality, I can trust that I will be okay.

Later in Nick Cave's song, 'Into Her Arms', he says:

"But I believe in Love
And I know that you do too
And I believe in some kind of path
That we can walk down, me and you
So keep your candles burning..."

I believe in Love too. We know her as Amitabha. Others give her different names. She is here to give us the strength to face our difficulties, and to comfort us. She will soothe our stings, and bring us balm.

With refuge we create Pure Lands

Resting in refuge takes us in the direction of Buddhahood, and Buddhas naturally create Pure Lands.

Our Pure Lands are likely to be more modest than Amitabha's, and we shouldn't underestimate the effect they might have on us and on those around us.

When we visit a place that is cared for, we have an experience of that care. It is the difference between a big chain restaurant and a quirky independent café run by a passionate foodie. It is spending time in a garden that has been loved into shape over decades.

As we deepen in refuge, we make the spaces around us more beautiful because we want to. We tidy away the big pile of clothes in the corner of our bedroom because it is offending our eyes. We bring in a shocking pink dahlia from the garden because we want to look at it while we eat our dinner. We clean the dust from the big Buddha in the garden alcove because we know he wants to be clean.

Objects take on a sacred quality, even workaday ones like trowels or toothbrushes or the little bug that got into the raspberry tub as you picked them and who is tricky to rescue. We say sorry to our phone when we drop it, and we apologise for wasting the carrots that have rotted in the fridge. We bow to the slugs.

When we take refuge, everything around us becomes sacred. Everything is lit up.

Paperweights and dirt

I was on my way out of the shop when my eyes were snagged by something glittery. I asked my friend Caroline to wait for me, and went over to investigate.

They were translucent sparkling jellyfish of different sizes, each suspended in glass. Each paperweight was the ergonomic shape of a cartoon rocket without the flames – they looked like they had an urge to leave the table and pulse off towards the ceiling. I placed the heft of one in my hand – what a cool, smooth, stroke-able surface – and admired the light as it played around the glass and the object inside. How did they make the jellyfish? How did they get them inside?

After a tortuous period of deciding whether to buy the baby jellyfish or the mummy jellyfish, I decided it was cruel to separate them, and brought both of them home. The larger is currently sitting on the windowsill of my office, and the smaller is in our living room, nestled beside the pleasingly spherical blue pottery lamp I've had for twenty years.

When I placed the larger one on the windowsill, something immediately became apparent. My windows were filthy. The panes were covered in smears and dust, and the frames between the double glass were scattered with flies and detritus.

Full disclosure: I am not a good cleaner. I had known about my windows for some time. We do a better job with the temple upstairs, but our flat has many a corner which is cobwebbed, dusty, or just unashamedly in need of a good clean. It's always been this way. Tidy is important to me, clean less so.

It just doesn't sit very high on my list of priorities, of which there are many.

Having said that, when I do get round to cleaning under the table or sweeping the stairs, I do feel better – satisfied, cleansed. I enjoy looking at the cleaner space, and knowing that I have given it some attention and care.

As soon as I set the jellyfish on my windowsill, I knew that I needed to clean the windows without delay. She sat there glimmering and floating, all clean lines and bubbles of light, and I wanted to show her off, to make her space nice, to worship her. And so I did.

This is how Buddhas work. When we set a Buddha on a shelf, we notice that the picture on the wall behind the rupa is wonky. We find ourselves placing a little vase of flowers next to it, or offering it a tiny red leaf. We get out the hoover, tidy away those piles of paper, redecorate the room. We bow before it when we enter the room and before we leave. We feel gratitude. Before we know it, we have a little Pure Land.

The light is streaming in through the clear windows as I finish writing this piece, illuminating the trailing golden tendrils of my jellyfish. Maybe I'll move her around the house to help me with the cleaning. Either way, I'm grateful for the golden shadow she casts, just like the Buddha.

On being the Buddha's gardener

This week I am having a break from seeing my psychotherapy clients and doing project work, and so my usually packed full days are more spacious. Kaspa and I have been catching up a little in the temple garden, which is reasonably large and which periodically threatens to overwhelm us.

I forget that I enjoy gardening. When I'm busy with my work, I can't imagine taking time out to get into different clothes and fetch the trug and trowel from the shed at the top corner of the garden. I can't imagine leaving my cosy office and walking out into the chilly or drizzly air.

Some of what holds me back from engaging with the garden is a fear of a lack of competence. We are both amateurs when it comes to gardening. Until I wrote a novel about a gardener some years ago, I knew nothing about gardens and I wasn't very interested in them. My research included interviewing lovely old gardeners, learning the names of plants, reading about flowers and visiting beautiful gardens around the country. When we first moved in here and we had volunteers who knew much more than we did, and I was afraid of getting it wrong and seeming like a fool.

As I actually engage with the work, I remember that I can make a difference to how the garden looks. I can weed the vegetable patch and use the secateurs to snip off all the spent flower heads. I can move the existing peonies and pinks around in this flower bed like rearranging furniture, and make a decision about where to place the new rose campion. I can even wield the electric hedge trimmer! I will continue to make mistakes, but this is how we learn, and in a garden even the worst losses are eventually redeemable.

By the end of the week, I felt immensely satisfied with how different the garden looked. Yes, there is still a lot to do, but that is the nature of living here. I trust that I or others will contribute their time in the future to tackle the long weedy bed at the bottom, and the many tangled and brambly corners that need attention. If they don't, well – those areas of the garden will just stay messy.

The best thing about being out in the garden is knowing that I am tending it for the Buddha. I feel this especially when I am working close to one of our garden rupas – spreading rich compost around the bright red geraniums at the feet of the stone wall Buddha, or sweeping leaves from the arch where the big Buddha lives. All the work I do in the garden is for the Buddha, and for this temple, and for the people who use it. I know that it makes the Buddha happy to see anyone taking care of anything – and it makes me happy to know that I'm making him happy.

At my best, all the work I do is an offering to the Buddha – writing this book, cleaning the cat bowls, sending birthday cards, thanking whoever has volunteered to wash up the mugs after our Buddhist services. When I catch myself feeling resentful about this job or that, it helps to remember that I'm not really doing it for myself. If it's all an offering, then it doesn't matter if we get what we think we want in return or not. The garden is a place where I learn about myself, and reconnect with the earth. It is where I make small rearrangements of living things on the garden Buddha's shrine. It is where I am given so much – the sweet scent of our luscious roses, long-tailed tits bombing the bird feeder, the puddle of dainty pale pink cyclamen, tadpoles clotting our pond, the dark magic of homemade compost, the sound of rain from the cosy dry alcove – all of it grace.

Rearranging the furniture

Yesterday Kaspa and I returned from a week's holiday in Yorkshire, where we walked across the moors and watched Project Runway on the television and ate vegan cake.

When we go away, we often talk about the shape of our lives from a greater distance – how the temple is doing, what we might want to change, and how we are doing as individuals. We did this as we drove through the heather-covered hills and sat at the kitchen table in our little cottage. We had time to think as we listened to talks by Richard Rohr and explored new towns.

Last night we were exhausted after the long drive home to the temple, but as we looked around our living room with our post-holiday eyes we had the idea of rearranging our furniture.

We lugged sofas, armchairs, tables, Buddhas and bookshelves from one place to another. We kept at it for an hour and a half, as it got later and later, and we could not get it to work. Should we get rid of a sofa? Buy a new table? How about if we put that there, and then that could go over there...

Our week away allowed lots of internal furniture rearranging. I had fresh thoughts about my new Buddhist group, my work-life balance, God, and my patterns in friendships. Some of these thoughts will lead to changes in my outside world (some already have), and some will continue to simmer away until the time is ripe.

Sometimes we need to get away from our everyday lives to allow the furniture in our head to move about. This process can be scary – it exposes dust balls, creates chaos, and for a while we don't know if the furniture will find a new good place or if it'll leave us in a worse place than before.

Once it's shifted, we may find that we want to change our environment as a natural consequence of the changes. We are likely to change our surroundings in the direction of less clutter, more openness and more beauty. We may also find ourselves including more of our character in our surroundings, letting go of things other people have given us or the way we think things 'ought' to look, and enjoying new quirky details.

Our furniture finally all fitted into perfect new places. We opened up the view to the garden, and the whole room felt more spacious and light. The golden Buddha that sat on the shrine at our wedding came into the centre of the new space. We've also let go of lots of objects that no longer belong with us – they're off to the charity shop. I am sitting on one of our sofas in its new position, pointing towards the garden. When I look around, I see the Pure Land. I am happy.

With refuge we surrender

I have been told that the universe is one gigantic benign unfolding. I have also been told that the universe can't be trusted, and that we need to protect ourselves from it and from other people.

I choose to believe in the former – a benevolent universe, which is moving very slowly towards good. It has created the intricacy of alveoli, pale creatures in the heavy dark deep sea, the giant redwood. It has created the night sky. It has created you.

Choosing to see the universe in this way helps me to live a happier life, a life where I can relax and let myself be carried by the currents.

Relaxing into these currents is taking refuge.

Surrendering isn't giving up or opting out. Sometimes it is necessary to swim against the currents, and the currents are strong. Surrendering is listening out for when we should be pushing, and when we should be letting go, like childbirth. It is trusting that there is a bigger process at work which we have no idea about. It is being led.

Surrender can feel delicious, especially if we have been fighting all our lives.

Trust surrender. It will carry you towards refuge. It will carry you home.

The paradox of self-power surrender

As I walk with my cup of tea to my laptop, I find myself chanting the nembutsu. It's the tune I use for my five minutes of daily practice every morning, and the one we use during prostrations, first raising our folded palms to our foreheads, mouths and hearts and then kneeling with our palms up, lifting the Buddha above ourselves.

This morning the tune arises naturally and I find myself wanting to sing it. It isn't always this way. Like many of the habits that keep me healthy, I find that there is an element of will power involved in setting them up and keeping them going.

It feels a bit risky to say this as a Pureland Buddhist. Sometimes the rhetoric is that we don't have any power ourselves, and so we just need to lean completely into Amitabha and let her work through us.

In my experience, sometimes I need to intervene to get myself onto the yoga mat or to open a spreadsheet. Maybe my will power is all Amida's work, maybe not, but it does have the feeling of a part of me nudging another part, rather than something that comes from outside of me.

When I do take these steps to begin and maintain healthy habits, like spiritual practice, nature walks or yoga, I do find myself closer to the Buddha – and then everything starts to feel easier. I have a sense of life flowing, I feel calmer, and I feel more able to meet the challenges ahead of me.

Rami Shapiro, in his book 'Recovery', speaks of the necessity of turning our faces towards the light. I like to think of self-power and other-power as working in tandem – we get some sense of the 'right thing to do', we encourage ourselves to do it, and then we feel the Buddha take her own step in the dance. We lean into the Buddha and enjoy being swept around the dance floor.

I think that the Buddha needs us to make the first move. I think she would love to dance with us, and is standing just at the edge of the dance floor, trying to catch our eye.

What the Buddha doesn't want is to force us. We need to be willing. We need to 'put in the footwork'. Taking refuge can come from this 'self-power' place, especially as we begin – we do it regardless of whether we want to or not, and whether or not it seems to be working. As they say in the 12 step programmes, we 'fake it to make it'.

As time goes on, we notice that we are feeling different. We find the nembutsu arising in our minds naturally, and we chant it because we want to. We get to know the feeling of leaning into the Buddha as we whirl round the dancefloor, and we trust that she won't let us go.

Desperation as a door to grace

When I walked into my first 12 step meeting, I was desperate. Most people need to reach a level of desperation before they get to their first meeting – this is also true of clients that come to see me as a psychotherapist. Nobody really wants to pay money to tell a professional how miserable they are, or how they're messing things up. In a similar way, nobody wants to admit to a room full of strangers that their addiction has brought them to their knees.

If I try to remember what happened in that first meeting, many years ago, I can only really remember being made a cup of tea, and lots of things I didn't understand being read from various books. I can also remember the strange echoing of names that happens in meetings. 'Hi, I'm John and I'm an addict.' Everyone else in unison: 'Hi John.' I can't remember if I spoke or not. I can't remember much of what I said at all in that first year of learning.

What I can remember is how happy some of the people in the group seemed. They had an unusual quality that I couldn't put my finger on – they seemed to take life lightly, and they laughed a lot. They also displayed a kind of confidence, even when things were going terribly for them. I now know this to be faith, but at the time it was a mystery. I baulked at the mentions of God and a Higher Power (whatever that meant), but bit by bit I trusted the advice I was given. I tried it out for myself and I began to transform.

Having arrived on my knees, it wasn't such a stretch to bow all the way down to the floor and put something above me.

To begin with, the 'something above me' was the wisdom of the group, as I grudgingly entertained the idea that the group might know more than I did about my problem and what I should do about it. I surrendered to the process of the group, keeping an open mind about what I needed to hear and who might say it. I found more and more that the world did indeed seem to know what was good for me, and that if I kept my ears and eyes open I would receive what I needed exactly when I needed it.

In order to receive something, we have to be able to empty ourselves out first. We need to dismantle some of our preconceptions and beliefs, or at least make some cracks in the walls. In order to do this, we need to trust that we will be looked after. We need to prostrate ourselves on the floor, showing the back of our necks to our enemies, trusting that they will not use their swords.

Of course, being vulnerable helps us to surrender but it can also hinder our powers of discernment. When we're desperate, it's harder to know if what we're surrendering to is really healthy and helpful for us, or whether it's a group that wants to exploit us or control us. Even when we completely surrender, it is always helpful to keep one eye open. What are our friends and family thinking about what we're doing? Are we feeling better or worse? Are we being encouraged to think for ourselves as well as listen to the wisdom of others? Do we feel more free or less free?

The paradox of surrender is that sometimes even if we are afraid, we are called to go with it. We take steps into a new place, away from everything we know. Sometimes it takes desperation to force us away from our familiar but crumbling structures. I am more grateful than you can know for the difficulties that forced me into the meeting that day. It has brought me everything that is important in my life. Maybe your desperation and distress will take you through similar doors. The light is waiting.

The day I lost everything

I stepped onto the train platform and felt for the strap of my handbag. My rucksack was there. The present for my friend Heather was there. My tube ticket was there. Where was my handbag?

My handbag was gone.

I'd travelled early that morning from Malvern to Paddington, and taken the tube to Charing Cross on the way to my psychotherapy supervision training. I was half an hour away from the Tibetan Buddhist centre where the training would take place. Without my handbag.

I went into action mode. I ran after the disappearing tube to see if I'd left it on my seat – nothing. I walked quickly to find a tube employee, who sent me to the mainline station, who sent me to lost luggage, who said I'd have to call Paddington lost luggage. I racked my brains. Could I remember taking my handbag from the first train? I would rather it had been stolen, to save my embarrassment, but I had a horrible feeling...

As I walked from place to place, I was counting my losses. £160 in cash. My phone and all those phone numbers. My Kindle. My iPod. My bank cards, driving license, and all the cards in my wallet. My £70 train ticket home and travel cards for the weekend. My house keys. My Filofax, which contained my entire life – all my client appointments, all my addresses, my schedule for the entire year. Gone.

I asked the train staff if they could call Paddington for me – I had no money and no phone. My eyes pleaded with them. They said they couldn't help me. At this point, I realised that I had a choice. I was feeling more and more panicky. I could either burst into tears, schlep back to Paddington, cancel the weekend's training and go home with my tail between my legs. Or I could take one step at a time and go forwards. I went forwards. I carried on to my destination.

I arrived at my training (late) and announced to the group of strangers that I'd had a disaster. They were all wonderful. The centre director looked up numbers for me on his computer (Paddington lost property, my bank to cancel cards...), the course leader leant me money for lunch, my husband got in contact with my friend Heather to warn her I was uncontactable, I hogged the centre phone during the breaks and during lunch.

It wasn't an easy day. Waves of panic, sadness and anger passed through me. I felt utterly stupid, I was afraid of the unknown, I was in despair. I kept working with the feelings as they arose. I thought 'one step at a time' or 'it's only money and inconvenience, nobody is dying' or simply 'let go'. My gaze kept returning to the huge shrine in the room we were working in, and the three big golden Buddhas. I allowed myself to feel supported by the universe. I'd be looked after, one way or another. I was gifted faith.

By the time I stood under the clock at Waterloo station, waiting for my friend Heather, I felt better than okay. I felt good. I had truly given up on getting back the contents of my handbag. I thought they might recover my Filofax, if I was lucky. I had let go. I felt light, calm – invincible. As I waited for my friend, a man approached me.

"Are you Satya?"

"Yes?"

"I'm Pete. We've got your bag."

Pete and his partner had travelled from Malvern on my train that morning. They'd seen my bag left behind on my seat, and watched people walk past. They thought, 'we have to do something'. They took it to lost property, who told them they'd charge for me to collect it. And so they found my text to Heather on my phone, arranging when and where we were meeting. They'd been trying to get in touch with her all day to let her know that they had my bag. And then they'd COME TO MEET ME.

For the first time that day, the tears came. I hugged them both. I'd let go of it all – my Kindle, my Filofax, my phone, my iPod, all that much-needed cash. And here it all was. Returned to me – delivered to me on the other side of London – by strangers who wanted to do the right thing. I could hardly believe it.

On my way back from London yesterday, I read this:

"When we are forced to attend to the places where we are most stuck, such as when faced with our anger and fear, we have the perfect opportunity to go to the roots of our attachments. This is why we repeatedly emphasise the need to welcome such experiences, to invite them in, to see them as our path. Normally we may only feel welcoming towards our pleasant experiences, but Buddhist practice asks us to welcome whatever comes up, including the unpleasant and the unwanted, because we understand that only by facing these experiences directly

225

can we become free of their domination. In this way, they no longer dictate who we are." (Ezra Bayda, from 'Beyond Happiness')

I know this to be true. I let go, and I received everything.

Just As You Are

We end where we began.

If nothing else, I want you to finish this book knowing: Amida Buddha accepts you just as you are.

It doesn't matter if you can't feel it right now. It doesn't matter if you don't believe in Amida Buddha. It doesn't matter if you don't believe it is possible for anyone to really accept you exactly as you are now.

Amida will keep reaching out from her own side, whether or not you are ready to accept her. In the meantime, keep taking refuge.

The world is complicated, unfair, disappointing, terrifying and tragic. We all get old, get sick and die. There is no avoiding dukkha.

Knowing this, how can we not seek the Dharma? How can we not seek companions on the path? How can we not seek a guide?

For refuge I go to Amitabha, the Buddha of Infinite Light.
Namo Amitabhaya.

For refuge I go to the Buddha, the one who shows me the way in this life. Namo Buddhaya.

For refuge I go to the Dharma, the way of understanding and love. Namo Dharmaya.

For refuge I go the Sangha, the community that lives in harmony and awareness. Namo Sanghaya.

For refuge I go to the Pure Land, the perfect field of merit. Namo Buddhakshetraya.

May the nembutsu open you up to the infinite light. May you come home. Namo Amida Bu.

Where next

If you are interested in experimenting with a short daily nembutsu practice, there is a free email course here: www.amidamandala.com/30days.

You can read more about Amida Shu and about our form of Buddhism at www.amidashu.org (and see the reading list below). You can also see if there is a group near you, or read about starting your own. We also offer various resources for people who want to connect with us online.

You can read more about Amida Mandala, the temple I run with my husband Kaspa, here: www.amidamandala.com.

My own website with information about my writing and my therapy practice is at www.satyarobyn.com.

Glossary of terms

Amida Buddha – the Buddha of unlimited light and unlimited life. Shakyamuni Buddha told the story of Amida Buddha who is said to have existed many millions of years before Shakyamuni.

Amida Shu – the name of a new school of Pureland Buddhism in the West, inspired by many of the great Pureland ancestors and founded by Dharmavidya David Brazier.

Amitabha (Sanskrit) – the Sanskrit word for Amida Buddha, which means Buddha of infinite light.

Amitayus (Sanskrit) – an alternative name for Amida which means Buddha of infinite life.

Avalokiteshvara (Sanskrit) – the Sanskrit name for Quan Shi Yin, the Bodhisattva of Compassion. Quan Shi Yin is one of Amida's attendants, along with Tai Shi Chih.

Bodhisattva (Sanskrit) – Bodhisattvas are inspired by the Buddhas and, although not yet Buddhas themselves, have great compassion and dedicate themselves to helping all sentient beings.

Bombu (Japanese) – a foolish being of wayward passion. As bombu beings we put ourselves in relationship with Amida Buddha and trust that if we say the nembutsu our rebirth in the Pure Land is guaranteed.

Buddha (Sanskrit) – an enlightened being. Commonly used to mean Shakyamuni Buddha, the historical Buddha, who lived in India around 2500 years ago.

Buddhakshetra (Sanskrit) – literally 'Buddha field', also known as a Pure Land. This is the field of influence around a Buddha. Devout Buddhists pray to be reborn in a Pure Land which is the perfect place to learn and practice the Dharma. See also: Pure Land and Sukhavati.

Contrition – a deep feeling of regret and sadness when we fully realise the harmful consequence of our actions, whether intended or otherwise.

Dharma (Sanskrit) – fundamentals. Hence, (a) the teaching of Buddha, (b) real things, as opposed to mere appearance. One of the three jewels.

Dukkha (Sanskrit) – affliction or suffering. The first of the four noble truths.

The four noble truths – the first teaching the Buddha gave and one that he repeated throughout the decades of his Dharma. For Dharmavidya's interpretation of the four noble truths see his book, 'The Feeling Buddha'.

Honen Shonin – (1133–1212) a Japanese Buddhist sage and the founder of Jodo Shu, the first Independent Pureland school in Japan.

Jodo-Shu (Japanense) – the school of Buddhism founded by Honen Shonin.

Jodo-Shinshu (Japanese) – the school of Buddhism founded by Shinran Shonin, one of Honen's disciples. Currently the largest Pureland school in Japan.

Karma (Sanskrit) – the Buddhist idea that all intentional actions sow seeds that ripen in the future, either as internal mental states or as worldly circumstances.

Mahayana Buddhism – one of the two main branches of Buddhism (the other is Theravada) practised widely in China, Japan, Korea, Tibet and Taiwan. Made up of a collection of Buddhist schools including Zen, Tibetan and Pureland Buddhism.

Mappo – 'the degenerate age' following the fading away of the influence of the Buddha's teachings.

Minister – a fully ordained Buddhist priest in Amida Shu.

Namo Amida Bu (anglicised Japanese) – the nembutsu, or saying the name of Amida Buddha. In Japan, Pureland Buddhists mostly say Namu Amida Butsu, and in China they say Namo Omito Fo.

Nembutsu (Japanese) – the practice of saying 'Namo Amida Bu'. In the Larger Pureland Sutra it says that anyone who hears the name of Amida Buddha will be reborn in his Pure Land. Honen asks us to recite the nembutsu so it is audible to our own ears.

Pali – the language in which the scriptures of the Theravada School of Buddhism are recorded.

Precepts – ethical ideals such as 'do not kill' which we aspire to as Buddhists. Ordained people in the Amida Order take a number of precepts in their Ordination ceremony and make a formal vow to keep them as best they can.

The Pure Land – see Buddhakshetra. Generally, in Pureland Buddhism, this refers to the realm of bliss that surrounds Amida Buddha. This is described in great detail in the Larger Pure Land Sutra. Some Amida Shu Buddhists see the Pure Land as a real place where they will be reborn after death. Others see it as a vision of an ideal society where we care for each other and the environment, and which we can start working towards right now in this life.

Pureland Buddhism or just Pureland – the form of Buddhism popularised by Honen in the 12th century in Japan, based on the vows made by Amida Buddha.

Quan Shi Yin (Chinese) – the Bodhisattva of Compassion, also known as Avalokiteshvara.

Refuge – taking refuge is a central practice for all Buddhists and gives us a sense of security and faith. Most Buddhists take refuge in the three jewels – Shakyamuni Buddha, the Dharma and the Sangha. Amida Shu Buddhists also take refuge in Amida Buddha and in the Pure Land.

Rupa (Sanskrit) – the power that an object has to draw our attention, or an object that is highly charged with personal meaning. We also speak of Buddha statues as being 'Buddha rupas' as they represent the Buddha.

Samsara (Sanskrit) – the continuing cycle of birth and death, the world of karma, and the worldly world.

Sangha (Sanskrit) – the community of people who follow the Buddha's teachings. One of the three jewels.

Sanskrit – the language of Indian Mahayana Buddhists texts.

Shakyamuni Buddha – literally 'sage of the Shakyas'. The Buddha (born as a prince, Siddhartha Gautama) who lived 2500 years ago in India and who founded Buddhism as a religion.

Sukhavati (Sanskrit) – literally 'sweet or blissful land', also known as the Pure Land.

Sutra (Sanskrit) – the sacred scriptures that contain the discourses of the Buddha (Sutta in Pali).

The Three Jewels – the Buddha, the Dharma and the Sangha. In our school of Buddhism we add Amida Buddha and the Pure Land to this list.

Recommended reading

I'd suggest that you begin with the starred books.

'The Big Book' and all related 12 step literature (or even better, go to an open 12 step meeting or find one that suits your own preferred addiction).

Bloom, Alfred *Essential Shinran: The Path of True Entrusting* (2006) World Wisdom Books

Bikkhu Bodhi (Translator) *The Connected Discourses of the Buddha: A Translation of the Samyutta Nikaya* (2003) Wisdom Publications

Bikkhu Bodhi (Translator) *The Numerical Discourses of the Buddha: A Complete Translation of the Anguttara Nikaya (Teachings of the Buddha)* (2012) Wisdom Publications

Brand, Russell *Recovery: Freedom from our Addictions* (2017) Bluebird

Brazier, Caroline *The Other Buddhism: Amida Comes West* (2007) O Books

Brazier, David *Buddhism Is A Religion* (2014) Woodsmoke Press

Brazier, David *Love and its Disappointment* (2009) O Books

Brazier, David *Not Everything Is Impermanent* (2013) Woodsmoke Press

* Brazier, David *Questions in the Sand* (2017) Woodsmoke Press

* Brazier, David *The Feeling Buddha: A Buddhist Psychology of Character, Adversity and Passion* (2002) Robinson

Brazier, David *Who Loves Dies Well* (2007) O Books

Brazier, David *Zen Therapy: Transcending the Sorrows of the Human Mind* (1995) New York: John Wiley & Sons

Fitzgerald, Joseph A. *Honen the Buddhist Saint: Essential Writings and Official Biography* (2006) World Wisdom Books

Holmes, Tom *Parts Work: An Illustrated Guide to Your Inner Life* (2007) Winged Heart Press

Keenan, Terrance *Zen Encounters With Loneliness* (2014) Wisdom Publications

Bikkhu Nanamoli (Translator) Bikkhu Bodhi (Translator) *The Middle Length Discourses of the Buddha: A Translation of the Majjhima Nikaya (Teachings of the Buddha)* (1995) Wisdom Publications

May, Gerald *Addiction and Grace: Love and spirituality in the healing of addiction* (2007) Bravo Ltd.

May, Gerald *The Awakened Heart: Opening yourself to the love you need* (1993) HarperOne

Paraskevopoulos, John *Call of the Infinite: The Way of Shin Buddhism* (2009) Sophia Perennis et Universalis

Robyn, Satya *What Helps: Sixty Slogans to Live By* (2018) Woodsmoke Press

* Robyn, Satya and Thompson, Kaspalita *Just As You Are: Buddhism for Foolish Beings* (2015) Woodsmoke Press

Shapiro, Rami *Recovery - The Sacred Art: The Twelve Steps as Spiritual Practice* (2009) Skylight Paths Publishing

Suzuki, Shunryu *Zen Mind, Beginner's Mind* (2005) Weatherhill

Welwood, John *Toward a Psychology of Awakening: Buddhism, Psychotherapy, and the Path of Personal and Spiritual Transformation* (2002) Shambhala

Unno, Taitetsu *Shin Buddhism: Bits of Rubble Turn into Gold* (2002) Harmony

Unno, Taitetsu *River of Fire, River of Water* (1998) Image

Walshe, Maurice (Tr.), Sumedho, Ajahn (Foreword) *The Long Discourses of the Buddha: A Translation of the Digha Nikaya* (1995) Wisdom Publications

Printed in August 2021
by Rotomail Italia S.p.A., Vignate (MI) - Italy